...rld's longest established
...st-known travel brands,
...are the experts in travel.

...more than 135 years our
...ave unlocked the secrets
...ations around the world,
...th travellers a wealth of
experience and a passion for travel.

**Rely on Thomas Cook as your
travelling companion on your next trip
and benefit from our unique heritage.**

Thomas Cook **pocket** guides

ST LUCIA

Written and updated by Polly Thomas
Original photography by Polly Thomas and Dexter Lewis

Published by Thomas Cook Publishing
A division of Thomas Cook Tour Operations Limited
Company registration no. 3772199 England
The Thomas Cook Business Park, Unit 9, Coningsby Road,
Peterborough PE3 8SB, United Kingdom
Email: books@thomascook.com, Tel: +44 (0) 1733 416477
www.thomascookpublishing.com

Produced by Cambridge Publishing Management Limited
Burr Elm Court, Main Street, Caldecote CB23 7NU
www.cambridgepm.co.uk

ISBN: 978-1-84848-455-9

First edition © 2009 Thomas Cook Publishing
This second edition © 2011
Text © Thomas Cook Publishing
Maps © Thomas Cook Publishing/PCGraphics (UK) Limited

Series Editor: Karen Beaulah
Production/DTP: Steven Collins

Printed and bound in Spain by GraphyCems

Cover photography © Danielle Devaux/4Corners

CONTENTS

WHAT'S IN YOUR GUIDEBOOK?

Independent authors Impartial up-to-date information from our travel experts who meticulously source local knowledge.

Experience Thomas Cook's 165 years in the travel industry and guidebook publishing enriches every word with expertise you can trust.

Travel know-how Thomas Cook has thousands of staff working around the globe, all living and breathing travel.

Editors Travel-publishing professionals, pulling everything together to craft a perfect blend of words, pictures, maps and design.

You, the traveller We deliver a practical, no-nonsense approach to information, geared to how you really use it.

ABOUT THE AUTHOR

Polly Thomas is a freelance writer and editor who first travelled to the Caribbean aged 17. Since then she has visited most of the islands, and is author of guidebooks to Jamaica and Trinidad & Tobago, as well as numerous articles on the region. She now lives in Trinidad with her partner and child.

● *The lofty palms and golden sand at Marigot Bay*

INTRODUCTION
Getting to know St Lucia

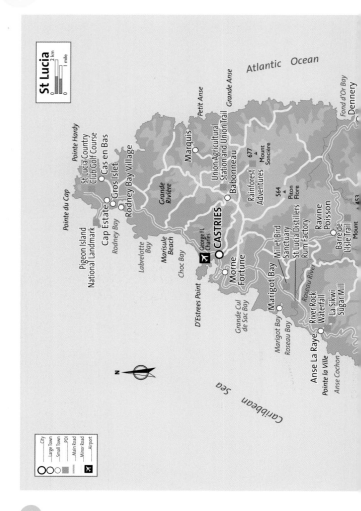

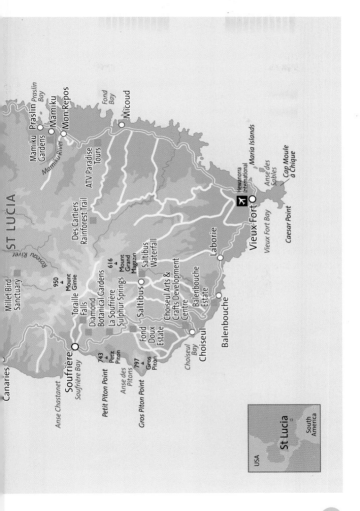

Getting to know St Lucia

With its fantastic scenery, lovely beaches and excellent tourism infrastructure, St Lucia is one of the most beguiling Caribbean destinations. Situated in the middle of the Lesser Antilles and to the north of the Windward Islands chain, teardrop-shaped St Lucia boasts some of the region's most spectacular landscapes, with the conical volcanic peaks of the **Pitons** soaring out of the Caribbean Sea and dominating the island's southwest.

The lowlands to the north are taken up with extensive groves of swaying banana plants, while the pretty little villages clinging to the slopes of the hilly interior are surrounded by carefully tended gardens of local vegetables, such as yam and dasheen, and swathes of lush rainforest, which support a diverse array of flora and fauna, including the brightly coloured St Lucia parrot. Waterfalls tumble out of the jungle throughout the island and offer some excellent swimming opportunities, while the thermal springs around Soufrière promise therapeutic bathing in warm, mineral-rich pools.

● *Castries, the capital, is a busy port*

St Lucia's coastline is equally varied, with the calm, warm waters of the Caribbean Sea lapping against a series of white-, yellow- and brown-sand beaches along the west coast, and the rougher Atlantic pounding the rugged shoreline of the east, where riptides and undercurrents make the beaches more attractive to nesting turtles than human swimmers. The tropical climate, meanwhile, ensures gorgeous sunshine year-round, with the heat tempered by cooling trade winds around Christmas and the odd shower of rain during the summer.

As you'd expect, the bulk of the tourism development is along the Caribbean west coast, with the main resort area, **Rodney Bay** in the northwest, spreading back from one of the island's best beaches and within easy distance of the vibrant capital, **Castries**. Rodney Bay has hotels aplenty alongside a host of tourist-oriented restaurants, bars and shops, and the liveliest nightlife scene on the island. St Lucia isn't really known as a party hotspot, however; in fact, it's one of the Caribbean's biggest honeymoon destinations, with a selection of lovely hotels that are popular with newly-weds for their privacy and intensely romantic ambience. Many of these are in the scenic surrounds of **Marigot Bay**, a protected little cove with a palm-shaded white-sand beach and a smart yachting marina; or in and around **Soufrière**, home of the Pitons, where guest rooms afford jaw-dropping views of the twin mountains.

The island is also renowned for its spas, which offer world-class service and make good use of their Caribbean location, with massage gazebos by the sea and treatment rooms with a view. And if you want to get active, St Lucia offers plenty of scope, from swinging through the forest canopy on a zipwire or taking a quad-bike tour, to hopping aboard a catamaran or classic sailing boat for a cruise down the coast and a spot of snorkelling over the dazzling reefs.

St Lucia's history

St Lucia was settled first by Amerindians from the South American mainland in around AD 200. By the mid-17th century, after a couple of failed attempts by British colonists, the French arrived and settled in earnest, establishing towns such as Soufrière and leaving behind a smattering of their language as well as a decidedly Gallic influence on the cuisine. The British were quick to challenge French rule, however, and numerous skirmishes took place between the two powers – their fierce desire to possess the island resulted in it becoming known as the 'Helen' of the West Indies, after the beautiful and equally fiercely coveted Helen of Troy.

Following several major skirmishes, such as the Battle of Cul de Sac in 1778, the British finally took control in 1848, ruling St Lucia as a crown

DUNSTAN ST OMER

Though Nobel Prize-winning playwright and poet Derek Walcott dominates St Lucia's cultural scene, the island has also produced some remarkable artists, whose work is easily accessible as you explore the sights. The most highly regarded among them is Dunstan St Omer, a close friend and contemporary of Walcott, whose striking murals featuring black saints and Madonnas adorn churches island-wide. Some of the best examples cover the walls of the huge Cathedral of the Immaculate Conception in Castries. Awarded the St Lucia Cross (the nation's highest award) in 2004 in recognition of his services to the country, and given a knighthood in 2010, St Omer has taught art in St Lucia for 30 years and is an inspiration to generations of young artists. However, he is perhaps best known locally as the designer of the national flag. Set on a cerulean blue background, which represents the Caribbean Sea, the flag features three triangles superimposed upon each other, reminiscent of the shape of the Piton mountains. The gold one symbolises the tropical sun, and the black-and-white ones symbolise the unity of the African and European influences on the island, although the black portion is deliberately larger in area to reflect the dominance of African-Caribbean culture.

🔺 *The Pitons, Soufrière*

colony until the island was granted independence in 1979. It now operates as a parliamentary democracy, with two main political parties vying for power. The plantation economy under the British saw the arrival of the African slaves whose descendants now make up the bulk of St Lucia's population and who are intensely proud of their Creole culture and language. Today, tourism is St Lucia's main economic earner, though the island also exports fruits such as bananas and mangoes as well as raw cocoa, which is used to make high-quality chocolate.

THE BEST OF ST LUCIA

St Lucia's attractions, from marvellous snorkelling to the truly awesome sight of the Pitons, are many and varied. The list below highlights the things that you can't afford to miss while on the island.

TOP 10 ATTRACTIONS

- **Pigeon Island National Landmark** With hiking trails, sweeping lawns and fabulous views of Rodney Bay, this is a great place for a walk or a picnic (see pages 40 and 42).

- **The Pitons** Rearing up from the Caribbean Sea, these startling conical peaks are the iconic image of St Lucia, equally beautiful from the water or from land (see page 56).

- **Canopy tour** This gondola trip suspends you 100 m (328 ft) above the rainforest for a wonderful perspective of the canopy; the zipwire swings add some thrills (see pages 85 and 87).

- **Diamond Botanical Gardens** Stroll around these lush manicured gardens, then take to the therapeutic waters of a hot mineral spring (see page 55).

- **La Soufrière Sulphur Springs** The bubbling, sulphurous pools of this 'drive-in volcano' offer a unique window into St Lucia's geological origins (see pages 56–7).

- **Snorkelling and diving** With stunning reefs and world-class dive sites, St Lucia's underwater world is a truly magical place (see pages 101–2).

- **Lunch with a view** Enjoy a gourmet meal at Ladera resort or the tasty set lunch at La Haut Plantation, all in the shadows of the Pitons (see pages 60 and 63).

- **Rodney Bay nightlife** With a string of open-air bars and some brilliant clubs, Reduit Beach Avenue is the island's nightlife hotspot (see page 32).

- **Fish fries** Fish and seafood are the dishes of the day at the Anse La Raye and Dennery events, all served up to the strains of soca and reggae (see pages 52, 78 and 80).

- **Boat cruise** Cruise down the coast from Rodney or Marigot bays to get spectacular views of the coastline and the Pitons (see page 98).

Plantation buildings at the Fond Doux plantation

SYMBOLS KEY
The following symbols are used throughout this book:

ⓐ address **ⓣ** telephone **ⓕ** fax **ⓦ** website address **ⓔ** email
ⓛ opening times **ⓘ** important

The following symbols are used on the maps:

𝒊	information office	**✝**	church
✉	post office	**O**	city
🛍	shopping	**O**	large town
✈	airport	**○**	small town
✚	hospital	**■**	point of interest
🛡	police station	**—**	main road
🚌	bus station	**—**	minor road

❶ numbers denote featured cafés, restaurants and evening venues

> ### RESTAURANT CATEGORIES
> The symbol after the name of each restaurant listed in this guide
> indicates the cost of a typical three-course meal without drinks
> for one person:
> £ under EC$50 ££ EC$50–80 £££ over EC$80

▶ *A beach resort at Vieux Fort*

RESORTS
Places under the sun

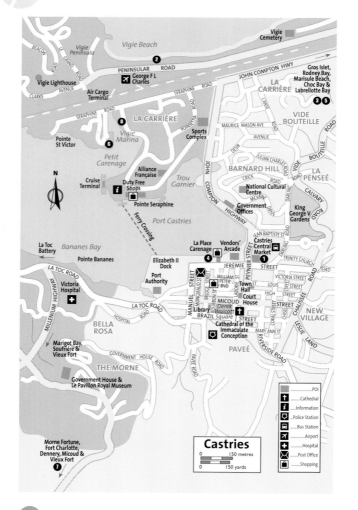

Castries

| | 0 | 150 metres |
| | 0 | 150 yards |

	POI
☩	Cathedral
ℹ	Information
▣	Police Station
▤	Bus Station
✈	Airport
✚	Hospital
✉	Post Office
🛍	Shopping

Castries

Busy and workaday, Castries town centre doesn't have many designated tourist attractions, but it does provide a sense of St Lucian life away from the resorts. Spreading back from the calm waters of Port Castries, with the cruise-ship dock and twin duty-free shopping emporia of Pointe Seraphine and La Place Carenage lying opposite each other on the two sides of the harbour, the city is overlooked by the leafy hills of Morne Fortune and Morne Pleasant, with grand residences old and new dotted between the trees. Much of the architecture of downtown Castries is modern, a rash of uninspiring concrete blocks that sprang up to replace the colonial-era wooden buildings destroyed during the fires in 1927 and 1948 that razed most of the town; a few gems do remain, however, particularly around the cathedral along Micoud Street. For Castries' answer to urban bustle, head for William Peter Boulevard, lined with banks and shops.

BEACHES

South of Castries, the coastline is taken up with the Hess Oil processing plant, so the best places to swim are north of town. A short way from the downtown area, the Castries–Gros Islet Highway runs parallel to part of **Choc Bay**, a lovely and undeveloped stretch of yellow sand and calm waters that can get packed on cruise-ship days, when passengers are ferried in to spend the day there. Drinks and meals are available from **The Wharf** restaurant (see page 25), at the Castries end of the beach; there's also a volleyball net here, and there are beach chairs for rent. The next accessible beach, **Marisule**, is reached via the left-hand turn-off from the highway, opposite the signposted right-hand turn (and traffic lights) for Grand Rivière. It's a pretty spot, though more of a fishing beach than a place to swim; for that, go around the headland to **Labrelotte Bay**, reachable via the next left, signposted for the Windjammer Landing resort. The hotel has guests-only sun loungers set up on the sands, but anyone's welcome to swim in the calm water or get a drink or meal at the resort's bars and restaurants (see page 25).

Downtown Castries

THINGS TO SEE & DO

Castries Central Market

Located in a prime position overlooking the city's harbour and right on the main road into town, Castries Central Market is a visual feast. Expect to see piles of artistically arranged fruits and vegetables – from prickly soursops and pineapples to misshapen tubers of yam, dasheen and eddo – presided over by inimitable female vendors. The front of the market is taken up with restaurants, shops and craft stalls laden with basketry, jewellery, trinkets and T-shirts. However, the real action is in the open-air section at the back, where to the side of the vegetable section, cuts of meat hang alongside glistening wheelbarrows of fresh sprats and huge sides of tuna and kingfish. The market is at its busiest on Saturday mornings, but is open on every day except Sundays. On the other side of the road, right on the waterfront, is the covered **Vendors' Arcade**, with a few stalls selling more local crafts.

ⓐ Corner of Peynier Street and Jeremie Street ⏱ 08.00–17.00 Mon–Sat, closed Sun

Cathedral of the Immaculate Conception

On the east side of Derek Walcott Square, the Cathedral of the Immaculate Conception is the island's main Catholic place of worship. It is an impressive building and is the largest church in the Caribbean, with enough room to seat some 2,000 people. Construction of the cathedral began in 1894 and was completed in 1931. However, today's structure sits on the site of several earlier churches, which were destroyed by fires. The cavernous interior is replete with colour, with paintings of various saints and the holy family, all of whom are depicted as being black. The paintings are by local artist Dunstan St Omer (a contemporary of Nobel Laureate Derek Walcott), who also designed the distinctive national flag (see page 10). There are more black saints in the stained-glass windows, and muted frescoes cover the ceilings.

ⓐ Corner of Laborie and Micoud streets ☎ 452 2271 ⏱ 09.00–17.00 daily; services 19.00 Sat, 06.00, 07.00 & (children's Mass) 10.30 Sun

ST LUCIA'S NOBEL LAUREATES

Despite its diminutive size, St Lucia has produced two Nobel Laureates, the most per capita of any country in the world and a feat of which its citizens are immensely proud. The first St Lucian to become a Nobel Laureate was Arthur Lewis (see page 22). The best-known recipient is the celebrated poet and playwright Derek Walcott, who scooped the Nobel Prize for Literature in 1992 and whom Salman Rushdie described as the 'greatest living English-language poet'. A giant of Caribbean literature, whose poetry gave voice to the frustrations and desires of Caribbean peoples in the post-independence age, Walcott was born in Castries in 1930, and grew up in a house on the capital's Chaussee Road; these days, he divides his time between the USA and St Lucia, where he has a home close to Pigeon Island. A prolific writer, Walcott has published more than 20 plays, but his finest works are his poems, such as the epic 1990 poem *Omeros*, a fantastical reworking of Homer's *Odyssey*, with the heroes as fishermen working the St Lucian waters, and his *White Egrets* collection, which scooped the T S Eliot Prize in 2011.

Derek Walcott Square

This landscaped oblong of green, named after the nation's Nobel Laureate, was formerly called Columbus Square and, before 1892, Promenade Square. It was originally laid out by the French, however, as the Place d'Armes, and had the requisite guillotine in place following the French Revolution. Today it's a peaceful spot, shaded by the sprawling limbs of a massive samaan tree, said to be 400 years old; its green lawns – sporting 'don't walk on the grass' signs – are intersected by a paved pathway. A covered colonial-era bandstand is used for the occasional concert; at the centre of the square stand busts of Walcott and fellow Nobel prizewinner Sir Arthur Lewis, and a war memorial flanking a non-functioning fountain.

Ⓐ Brazil Street/Bourbon Street/Micoud Street/Laborie Street

● *Colonial-era building, Morne Fortune*

La Toc Battery

Following the harbour around to the southwest, La Toc Road winds upward to La Toc Battery. A former British fort, it has been meticulously restored by its current owners with a view to accommodating day-trippers from the many cruise ships that dock in Castries harbour during the high season. Strictly speaking, visits are by appointment only, but the site is usually open when a ship is in port. Built in 1888, the fort still has its original 18-ton muzzle-loading cannon, as well as plenty of dimly lit tunnels and bunkers to explore. There are displays on the battles fought from here by the British and French, and a huge collection of antique bottles. The gardens surrounding the fort are attractively landscaped and afford gorgeous views down to the harbour.

ⓐ La Toc Road ① 452 7921 ② 09.00–15.00 officially by appointment only, but usually open if a ship is in port ① Admission charge

THE FIRST ST LUCIAN NOBEL LAUREATE

The first St Lucian to become a Nobel Laureate was Arthur Lewis, who was awarded the Economics prize in 1979 for his pioneering work on economic expansion and poverty in developing countries. A child prodigy, he left school at 14 having completed the entire curriculum, and went on to win a scholarship to study at the London School of Economics, eventually continuing to PhD level; in 1948 at just 33, he was made a full professor at the University of Manchester, the first black man in the UK to attain such a position. In 1959, he moved back to the Caribbean to take up the position of principal at the University of the West Indies' campus in Kingston, Jamaica; but by 1963 – the same year he was knighted by Britain's Queen Elizabeth II – he had moved to the USA, where he ended his working life at Princeton University. He died on 15 June 1991, and is buried in the grounds of the Morne Fortune college that bears his name (see opposite).

Morne Fortune

Providing a beautiful green backdrop to the southern side of Castries, Morne Fortune is reached by a snaking road that switchbacks upwards, overhung with bright clumps of bougainvillea and passing some grand residences including Government House, the official residence of the governor general. A palatial, white-painted affair, built in 1895, its **Le Pavillon Royal Museum** is open to visitors by appointment only (📞 452 2481 🕐 10.00–12.00, 14.00–16.00 Tues & Thur), with a small collection of documents and photographs relating to the history of the house. Halfway up the Morne Fortune road, a lay-by affords some gorgeous views down over the port; vendors – selling jewellery and crafts – set up stalls here to take advantage of the passing tourist trade.

The top of the hill is taken up with the fortifications of **Fort Charlotte**, now home to the landscaped grounds of the **Sir Arthur Lewis Community College**, St Lucia's seat of higher education. Named after the Nobel prize-winning economist, it's a lovely campus of restored red-brick military buildings set around sweeping lawns. Morne Fortune's fortifications were begun by the French in 1768, but the British took over in the mid-18th century and constructed a number of splendid buildings as well as the Inniskilling Monument, built to honour the efforts of the Royal Inniskilling Fusiliers, who won the mount from the French in a fierce battle in 1796. From the high ground surrounding the monument, you can see all the way to Pigeon Island and, on a clear day, the neighbouring island of Martinique.

Vigie Peninsula

Heading into Castries from the north, the John Compton Highway hugs the waterline, passing Pointe Seraphine to the right and affording sweeping views over to the container ships and wharves of the port; the distinctive white pyramid overlooking the water just north of the Pointe Seraphine shopping complex is the island headquarters of the Alliance Française. Before you enter the town proper, the road runs parallel to the runway of George F L Charles Airport, used mostly by small planes flying between the Caribbean islands. At the foot of the runway, the tarmac gives on to the white-painted tombs of the Vigie Cemetery. Beyond that, the runway is bordered by Vigie Beach, a calm swathe of brown sand shaded by sea-grape trees. Popular with local taxi drivers, it's more a spot to park up and chill out than to swim. Another right turn from the highway just by the airport along Seraphine Road takes you to a couple of the popular waterfront restaurants (see pages 25–6) that overlook the yacht berths of Vigie Marina. The peninsula is topped by the Vigie Lighthouse, from where there are excellent views along the coast to the north and south; nearby, you can also explore the ruins of a French-built powder magazine from 1784.

⬥ *Labrelotte Bay, north of Castries*

TAKING A BREAK

Castries Central Market £ ❶   The line of kiosk restaurants to the side of the market are some of the best places in the country to taste authentic St Lucian cooking, from hearty pepperpot to *roti* or spicy fish; it's cheap, hot and delicious. Go early, as lunch runs out by about 14.00.
ⓐ Jeremie St, Castries 🕒 07.00–18.00 daily

Vigie Beach £ ❷   Vendors at the beach facilities here do an excellent line in local food, from jerk chicken cooked on smoky barbecues to fried fish and *rotis*. Great for a last bite while waiting for a plane.
ⓐ Vigie Beach 🕒 10.00–late Mon–Sat, closed Sun

The Wharf £ ❸   Right on the beach, and a bit rough around the edges, but serving up reliable local and international fare – burgers, soups, salads and sandwiches, as well as *rotis* and Creole shrimp. Cocktails and beers from the bar, too. ⓐ Choc Bay, Castries–Gros Islet Highway
❶ 450 4844 🕒 11.00–21.00 daily

Caribbean Pirates £–££ ❹   Deservedly popular place with nautical décor, an open-air balcony overlooking the water, and a huge menu that includes local seafood specialities – anything from stewed blackfish (a kind of whale) to curried lobster – as well as fresh fish and pizzas.
ⓐ La Place Carenage Shopping Centre, Jeremie St, Castries ❶ 452 2543
🕒 08.00–19.00 Mon–Thur, 08.00–23.00 Fri & Sat, closed Sun

Jammer's Beach Bar ££ ❺   Archetypal Caribbean restaurant, with beachside tables shaded by palms. Great for a light lunch (burgers, steaks, curried fish) or a frosty drink in the day, and equally good at night, when fairy lights strung up in the trees add a romantic atmosphere. Enjoy live music several evenings a week. Also, the adjacent Dragonfly restaurant is an excellent choice on Tuesdays, when there's a Caribbean-themed buffet. ⓐ Windjammer Landing, Labrelotte Bay
❶ 456 9000 🕒 11.00–22.30 daily

AFTER DARK

The Coalpot £££ 6 Extremely popular place for a special dinner, set right at the waterside and with charming rustic décor. Seafood is the name of the game: start with Coquilles St Jacques or fish chowder, then choose a sauce for your fish, lobster or shrimp. Those on offer include mushroom, Creole, coconut curry and garlic. ⓐ Vigie Marina ⓣ 452 5566 ⓦ www.coalpotrestaurant.com ⓛ 12.00–15.00, 17.00–late Mon–Fri, dinner only (17.00–late) on Sat, closed Sun

Green Parrot £££ 7 In a gorgeous setting with views down to the capital, this is a great place for a splurge, presided over by charismatic chef Harry Edwards, who trained at Claridge's. Ladies eat free on Mondays if wearing a flower in their hair and accompanied by a 'well-dressed' man (jackets required), and there's usually live entertainment on Wednesday and Saturday nights. ⓐ Morne Fortune ⓣ 452 3399 ⓛ 07.00–late daily

Jacques Waterfront Dining £££ 8 Upmarket waterside restaurant with a tropical garden ambience. The food fuses Caribbean flavours and a distinct French influence. Highlights on the menu include the seafood brochette and beef fillet with a green peppercorn and brandy sauce. Also known as 'Froggie Jacques', this place is across the water from the Coalpot, and has less of a crowd but much better views. ⓐ Vigie Marina ⓣ 458 1900 ⓦ www.jacquesrestaurant.com ⓛ 12.00–14.30, 18.00–late (last orders at 21.30) Mon–Sat, closed Sun

Rodney Bay

A rough triangle sandwiched between the sea and yacht marina, Rodney Bay Village is St Lucia's tourist honeypot, home to the majority of the island's places to stay, eat, drink and party, as well as its largest shopping centres. The main reasons for all this development are the fine white sands and calm waters of Reduit Beach, but the berths at the adjacent marina also keep things busy. The area has proved as attractive to locals as it is to visitors, with the hills overlooking the bay dotted with palatial homes, many of them owned by retired St Lucians who've moved home after years spent living abroad.

BEACHES

Reduit Beach

Bordered by the green-swathed outcrop of Labrelotte Point to the south and Pigeon Island National Landmark to the north, Reduit Beach is St Lucia's premier stretch of sand, much touted as the best beach in the island and certainly the busiest. Popular with cruise-ship visitors (who are bused in for the day), as well as regular tourists and locals, it's the closest St Lucia comes to a resort beach scene; you can rent a sun lounger or jet-ski, take a banana-boat ride or waterskiing lesson with the operators who work the crowds, or just spread out a towel and soak up the sun. There are a few places to grab a drink or a meal, the best of which is **Spinnaker's** (see page 31). Halfway up, the access channel for the Rodney Bay Marina runs between the beach and Gros Islet village.

THINGS TO SEE & DO

Rodney Bay Marina

With 232 slips set around a protected man-made lagoon, the Rodney Bay Marina is one of the best equipped in the region, and since 1991 it has served as the end point for the 200-plus vessels that take part in the annual Atlantic Rally for Cruisers, a punishing 2,700-nautical-mile (5,000-km) race

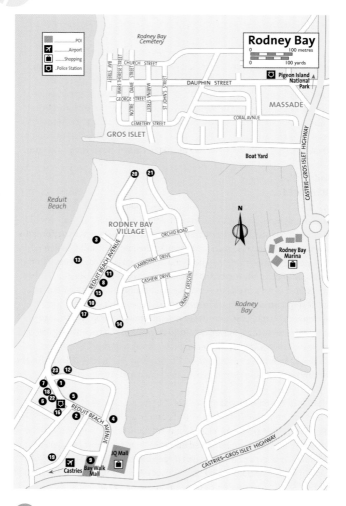

across the Atlantic from Spain's Gran Canaria. Having been bought by luxury developers ITG in 2007, the marina has just been treated to an upgrade, with enhanced offshore amenities and additional berths for mega-yachts. Set around a courtyard just off the main road, the marina's collection of shops and restaurants make a nice alternative to Rodney Bay proper. There is also a bank with an ATM and an Internet café. By road, the entrance to the marina is off the highway just north of the Rodney Bay turn-off, while the access channel for boats slices Reduit beach in half.

ⓐ Castries–Gros Islet Highway **ⓣ** 452 0324 **ⓦ** www.igy-rodneybay.com

Rodney Bay Village

From the Castries–Gros Islet Highway, the turn-off to Rodney Bay is marked by the JQ Shopping Mall, its 50-plus shops running from clothing boutiques to pharmacies and a large supermarket. Across the road, the smart new Bay Walk Mall has several international shops, from Hugo Boss to Benetton, plus a slew of restaurants, a Häagen Dazs outlet and a supermarket. Beyond the malls, Reduit Beach Avenue is the island's premier tourist strip, lined with hotels, bars and restaurants and at its liveliest after dark, when music blares from the open-air bars. Two large resorts block views to the beach, and if you're not staying on the sand, the easiest access to Reduit from the Avenue is adjacent to Spinnaker's restaurant (No 3 on map), where there's also a large car park. Side roads off from the Avenue to the east loop toward the waters of the Rodney Bay Marina.

TAKING A BREAK

If you're in the mood for some fast food, there is a branch of **Burger King** in JQ Mall, and a **Domino's** pizza outlet on Reduit Beach Avenue; for deliveries call **ⓣ** 458 0002 (closed Sun). For something more local in flavour, check out the vans parked opposite JQ Mall, selling spicy jerk chicken and open late to cater to partygoers. On the road to the right off Reduit Beach Avenue, past Big Chef (No 4 on the map), Elena's is the place for home-made ice cream in a delicious array of flavours.

Hotels on the coast offer fantastic sea vistas

The Lime £–££ ❶ A canteen-style lunch counter serving inexpensive local food (*roti*, fish broth, curried chicken, etc), and a sit-down section offering tasty Caribbean fare: pumpkin soup, salads, Creole shrimp and the like. It is also popular and buzzing after dark, with a range of entertainment from live music to karaoke. ⓐ Reduit Beach Avenue ⓣ 452 0761 ⓛ 11.00–24.00 daily

Café Claude ££ ❷ Great little place set on an all-wood veranda, with a profusion of plants providing some cover from the Avenue. The coffee and breakfasts are excellent, as are lunch or dinner of grilled red snapper, roast duck with garlicky sweet-potato mash or pork stroganoff. ⓐ Reduit Beach Avenue ⓣ 458 0847 ⓛ 08.00–late daily

Spinnaker's ££ ❸ Everything you could want from a beachside restaurant: tables under a palm-thatched roof, friendly service and a chalkboard menu that's heavy on the seafoods and salads, plus burgers and delicious natural juices – try the tamarind. ⓐ Reduit Beach Avenue ⓣ 452 8491 ⓛ 09.00–23.00 daily

Big Chef £££ ❹ Just off the Avenue, this is an indoor, air-conditioned steakhouse serving USDA Angus Beef steaks, hand-cut and trimmed in-house and cooked up with a variety of sauces. There are also grilled fish and seafood, and good soups and salads. ⓐ Reduit Beach Avenue ⓣ 450 0210 ⓛ 17.00–22.30 Mon–Sat, closed Sun

Delirius £££ ❺ Very cool hangout on a decked open veranda, popular with a lively crowd of visitors and locals. Daily specials – from quiche to pumpkin soup – are chalked up on the blackboard, and there's an international-style menu of such things as chicken satay or jerk tuna. There's also an award-winning cocktail list. ⓐ Reduit Beach Avenue ⓣ 451 3354 ⓦ www.deliriusstlucia.com ⓛ 11.00–late Mon–Sat, closed Sun

Ti Bananne £££ ❻ Lovely Caribbean international restaurant just off the Avenue, set by a pool and bedecked with colourful murals. The flavoursome menu of regional favourites includes green fig and saltfish salad, or orange and ginger-glazed fish. There's also all-day breakfast at the attached Lil'Chef, with favourites such as eggs Benedict and fruit smoothies. ⓐ Reduit Beach Avenue ⓣ 4450 0210 ⓛ 07.00–22.00 daily

AFTER DARK

If you're after some nightlife, you'll find Reduit Beach Avenue is busiest from Thursday to Saturday; the best way of finding out what's on is just to take a stroll along the road and check out which of the venues has the crowd that night.

🔺 *The long stretch of white sand at Reduit Beach*

Restaurants

Triangle Pub £ ❼   Open-air bar that's a popular spot for karaoke, with regular drinks promotions, too. Simple meals such as barbecued chicken or grilled fish are also available, with food served until late. ⓐ Reduit Beach Avenue ⓣ 452 0334 ⓛ 18.00–late daily

Memories of Hong Kong ££ ❽   Reliable and busy Chinese restaurant set on an open-sided veranda overlooking the Avenue. All the staple noodle, seafood, poultry and meat dishes are included in the extensive menu, from crispy duck pancakes to chow mein dishes, tofu in black-bean sauce or Sichuan beef, and there are set meals too. ⓐ Reduit Beach Avenue ⓣ 452 8218 ⓛ Mon–Sat 17.00–23.00, closed Sun

Spice of India ££ ❾   Serving authentic Indian cuisine, with tables inside and out, this is a laid-back, informal place to sample delicious curries, plus excellent breads and specials cooked in a tandoor oven. ⓐ Bay Walk Mall, Reduit Beach Avenue ⓣ 458 4253 ⓛ 18.00–23.00 daily

Tequila Joe's ££ ❿   Open-air restaurant and bar, with a passable menu of Mexican staples. It's a buzzing, busy spot, perhaps best for a margarita or for the regular live entertainment, which ranges from local bands to fire-eaters and limbo dancers. ⓐ Reduit Beach Avenue ⓣ 484 3663 ⓛ 17.00–01.00 Sun–Thur, Fri, Sat 17.00–03.00

Buzz £££ ⓫   Set just back from the main road in an elegant, partly open-air setting, this is a consistently good and rather upmarket restaurant that still feels pleasantly laid-back. The food is delicious, and runs from potato-crusted red snapper to lamb shanks with harissa sauce; there's also a good pasta selection, including several vegetarian options. ⓐ Reduit Beach Avenue ⓣ 458 0450 ⓦ www.buzzstlucia.com ⓛ 17.00–22.30 Tues–Sun, closed Mon

The Charthouse £££ ⓬   Overlooking the waters of the marina, this is one of the best options in the area, with a simple but tasty menu of

⬥ Take to the water in a Sunfish sailing boat

pastas, steaks, ribs and lots of seafood: try the spicy shrimp or lobster salad. ⓐ Off Reduit Beach Avenue ⓣ 452 8115 ⓛ 18.00–22.30 daily

Chic £££ ⑬ Styled as one of Rodney Bay's most upmarket restaurants, this indoor, air-conditioned restaurant is a special occasion kind of place. You're welcomed with a glass of complimentary cava, the sommelier is on hand to assist with your choice of wine, and the menu of Caribbean fusion cuisine is excellent and beautifully presented. ⓐ Rex Royal Resort, Reduit Beach Avenue ⓣ 452 9999 ⓛ 19.00–21.45 daily

The Edge £££ ⑭ In-hotel waterfront restaurant open daily for breakfast, lunch and dinner, but best at night, when it's dramatically lit by flambeaux. The European fusion menu, dubbed 'Eurobbean fusion' by the award-winning head chef, is pricey but delicious, and includes sensational sushi. ⓐ Harmony Suites Hotel, Flamboyant Drive, Rodney Bay Village ⓣ 540 3343 ⓦ www.edge-restaurant.com ⓛ 08.00–11.00, 12.00–15.00, 18.30–23.00 (sushi bar is open 12.00–23.00) daily

Fire Grill and Lounge Bar £££ ⑮ Casual alfresco bistro with chic décor, serving grilled steak and fresh fish dishes, plus a wide selection of cocktails. There is also a barbecue and entertainment on a Sunday evening and jazz or blues music in the lounge bar. A mature alternative to the boisterous bars of Rodney Bay. ⓐ Reduit Beach Avenue ⓣ 451 4745 ⓛ 12.00–15.30 Mon–Fri, 12.00–16.00 Sunday, 18.00–23.00 daily

Ku De Ta £££ ⑯ Gorgeous setting, reached by a lamp-lit pathway off the Avenue and with classy Asian-style décor and tables inside and on the patio, this upmarket Thai restaurant cooks up some delicious food, from authentically flavoured *tom yum* soup to all the staple noodle and stir-fry dishes, and curries, too, all courtesy of a chef from Thailand. ⓐ Off Reduit Beach Avenue ⓣ 459 4968 ⓛ 18.00–22.00 daily

Razmataz £££ ⑰ Bedecked with all manner of rich reds and golds, and with an open veranda overlooking the Avenue, this is an excellent spot for north Indian food, with a range of authentic curries cooked up by a Nepali chef. Excellent, attentive service, and happy hour from 17.00 to 19.00. ⓐ Reduit Beach Avenue ⓣ 452 9800 ⓦ www.razmatazstlucia.com ⓛ 17.00–23.00 Wed–Mon, closed Tues

Bars & clubs

Caesars ⓲ Newish bar and nightclub with a Roman theme, staging regular party nights and drinks promotions. It is often packed with dancing locals, especially on the Saturday Ladies' Night, when women get in free. Food is available, too. ⓐ Reduit Beach Avenue ⓣ 384 5759 ⓛ 18.00–late daily ❗ Admission charge

Club Santic ⓳ An upmarket nightspot, with several rooms, including a lounge bar and full-blown dance floor with VIP area. DJs play an eclectic music selection for a well-dressed crowd. ⓐ Off Reduit Beach Avenue ⓣ 484 1617 ⓛ 21.00–late Thur–Sat, closed Sun–Wed ❗ Admission charge

Happy Day Bar ⓴ Tiny little open-air bar overlooking the ocean, where drinks flow thanks to an all-day happy hour. Good cocktails and a nice place for a drink and a dance under the stars. ⓐ Reduit Beach Avenue ⓛ 18.00–late daily

The Loft ㉑ This is a laid-back option for a night out, set right at the sea's edge and popular with a more mature crowd. Local DJs play island tunes and there are regular special events. ⓐ Reduit Beach Avenue ⓛ 22.00–late Fri & Sat, closed Sun–Thur ❗ Admission charge

Mango's Bar ㉒ Cute little roadside bar, good for a beer or a cocktail. ⓐ Reduit Beach Avenue ⓣ No phone ⓛ 12.00–late daily

Upper Level ㉓ Indoor place upstairs and opposite The Lime, this is an inexpensive nightclub, with a youngish crowd of locals and visitors dancing to a mix of hip-hop, R&B and soca. ⓐ Reduit Beach Avenue ⓣ 452 9350 ⓛ 22.00–late Fri & Sat, closed Sun–Thur ❗ Admission charge

● *Taking a stroll at the Pigeon Island National Landmark*

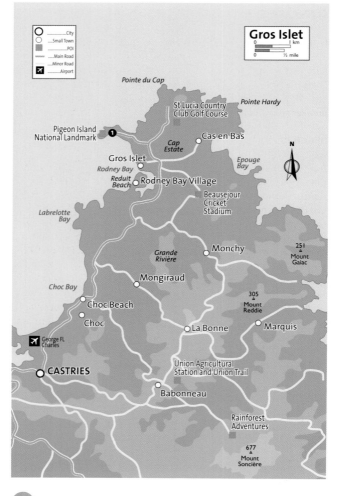

Gros Islet

Best known as the scene of the island's much-touted weekly
'jump-up' (see page 40), the fishing village of Gros Islet doesn't
have very much going on other than these Friday night festivities.
There is a pretty beach, however, which runs around the bay
towards the Pigeon Island National Landmark, one of St Lucia's
premier attractions.

BEACHES

From Gros Islet to Pigeon Island, a beach runs the length of Rodney Bay.
Dotted with nets drying in the sun and a fair bit of litter, the section in
front of the fishing village isn't a place to swim, but it gets a lot nicer –
and cleaner – north of the village, where it becomes Pigeon Island
Causeway beach. As you approach Pigeon Island, there is a smattering of
luxurious all-inclusive hotels built right on the sand. There's nothing to
say you can't use the northern half of the bay (all of St Lucia's beaches
are public up to the shoreline), but what with the patrolling security
guards and hotel paraphernalia, this end retains a private feel and is
pretty much the preserve of hotel guests only.

Pigeon Island itself has a couple of lovely places to swim, both quiet,
protected coves with changing facilities and toilets, though you do have
to pay the entrance fee to the park to use them (see page 40).

THINGS TO SEE & DO

Gros Islet

A marked contrast to the tourist facilities that dominate Rodney Bay
Village, Gros Islet's narrow streets spread back from the sea, and are
lined with private homes, many of them simple one-room constructions,
others with handsome gingerbread fretwork and wrap-around verandas.
Few tourists visit other than on Friday nights, when the village is
completely transformed by a huge street party.

THE FRIDAY NIGHT 'JUMP-UP'

Every Friday night, the streets are closed to traffic, and vendors set up stalls selling crafts and an array of delicious barbecued food, from *lambi* (conch), lobster and chicken to steamed fish. Soca and reggae blare from huge speakers, the drinks flow – sold from mobile bars and street-side establishments – and, by 22.00 or so, everyone's dancing on the tarmac in a cross-section of streets towards the beach. It's all pretty good-natured, though single women can expect plenty of attention from would-be dancing partners. It's best to leave expensive jewellery at home and, since parking can be difficult and you'll have to leave your vehicle a fair way away from the action, using taxis is the best option.

Across the Castries–Gros Islet Highway from the fishing village, Gros Islet extends inland towards the spanking-new Beausejour Cricket Stadium, completed in 2002 and used to stage one-day international and Test games; it also served as a venue for games during the 2007 Cricket World Cup and the 2010 T20 World Cup tournament.

Pigeon Island National Landmark

The distinctively twin-peaked landmass that forms the northern end of Rodney Bay, Pigeon Island is no longer an island at all, having been joined to the mainland by the construction of a causeway in the early 1970s, when mangroves were cleared and the area now taken up by the marina was dredged to make way for the ensuing tourism development. Today, the 16.2-ha (40-acre) park is owned and maintained by St Lucia's National Trust, and its lawns and footpaths are popular with locals and tourists alike; it also serves as one of the main venues for the annual Jazz Festival (see pages 103 and 105).

The island's history is not so pastoral, though; having been deserted by its first Amerindian inhabitants, said to be warlike Caribs, it became a pirate stronghold in the 16th century, when French-born buccaneer François Le Clerc (better known as Jambe de Bois because of

⬤ *The beach fringing Pigeon Island causeway*

his wooden leg) used it as a base from which to target passing ships; in 1554, he's said to have captured three galleons and held their crew to ransom.

The island's strategic position wasn't lost on the British, either. In the 18th century Admiral Rodney established a naval base in Gros Islet Bay and built fortifications all over Pigeon Island. It was from here that he launched the fleet that fought in the Battle of the Saintes, which took place over four days in April 1782 and which ended in a decisive victory for the British fleet, effectively ending French domination of the Caribbean. The island also served variously as a quarantine area and a whaling station. The remains of British-built fortifications are scattered all over the site; some have been fully restored – the Officers' Mess currently houses a restaurant and an Interpretation Centre with somewhat dated displays on the island's history – while others lie in picturesque ruins.

The main path through the park runs uphill to the most substantial of the fortifications, Fort Rodney. The short but steep climb to the fort provides panoramic views of Rodney Bay and over to the wilder northern coastline: you can see Martinique on a clear day. There's no trace of the huge wireless tower erected on top of the fort in the 1940s, when the American army commissioned the island as a naval station, but a rusting British cannon does remain. At the base of the fort, another path snakes off up the grassy Signal Peak, which affords more fine views over the island's northern tip.

ⓐ Pigeon Island ❶ 460 0603 ❷ 09.00–17.00 daily ❶ Admission charge

TAKING A BREAK

Captain's Cellar Pub £–££ ❶ Set in the brick-built cellars of the former British Officers' Mess, this is an atmospheric spot, cooled by constant breezes from the Atlantic and with tables indoors and out. Popular with expats, with a book exchange and regular events such as quiz nights, it has a simple lunch menu of baguette sandwiches, salads and *roti*, and more substantial English-style dishes such as bangers and

▲ *A solitary cannon at Fort Rodney*

mash with onion gravy, shepherd's pie, burgers, chilli con carne and baked potatoes. A nice place for a quiet drink, too. ❸ Pigeon Island ❶ 450 0918 Ⓦ www.captainscellarpub.com ⏰ 10.00–16.00 Mon & Sat, 10.00–23.00 Tues–Fri & Sun (Dec–Apr); 10.00–23.00 Tues–Fri & Sun, 10.00–16.00 Sat, closed Mon (May–Nov)

Marigot Bay

South of Castries, the west-coast highway swings past the giant silos and ugly moonscape of the Hess Oil Terminal on one side, and the waving fronds of the Cul de Sac Valley banana plantation on the other. The next valley to the south, Roseau, is also planted with bananas, but both took a beating from Hurricane Tomas in 2010, which all but destroyed the plantations. However, tourism has long taken over from agriculture as the main earner hereabouts. Most of the development centres on Marigot Bay, a gorgeous protected cove that's one of the most photographed in the Caribbean, with several hotels and restaurants as well as a handsome beach. South of Marigot, the Millet Bird Sanctuary offers pleasant respite from sun and sea, with trails to walk and excellent birdwatching.

THINGS TO SEE & DO

Marigot Bay

A barrage of signs advertising places to stay and eat mark the turn-off to Marigot Bay, St Lucia's second busiest resort after Rodney Bay and well worth a visit even if you're not staying there. Best known as the location for Rex Harrison's 1967 film *Doctor Dolittle*, the bay has a picture-perfect combination of forested hillside descending down to palm trees and azure waters, perhaps best appreciated from the lookout point above the bay, where a bar has been set up to cater to passing visitors. Down at the bay proper, upmarket resorts are hunkered into the hillsides, while the waterfront holds the upmarket Marina Village, a complex of smart boutiques (and a café and bank) built in classic Caribbean style, with fretworked balconies and wooden decking overlooking the water, and luxury yachts bobbing at the marina's moorings. From the jetty, water-taxis will take you across the bay to the thin spit of palm-shaded sand in front of the Marigot Bay Beach Club; there's good snorkelling to the western side of the beach, and watersports are available from the Marigot Beach Club (W www.marigotbeachclub.com).

○ Taking a boat trip at Marigot Bay

Millet Bird Sanctuary

Centred around the Roseau Dam, one of the largest in the eastern Caribbean, the Millet Bird Sanctuary is home to more than 30 species of birds, including five endemic species – the St Lucia Parrot, St Lucia Oriole, St Lucia Finch, St Lucia Warbler and St Lucia Peewee – the most distinctive being the flashy St Lucian Oriole. As it's a protected reserve, you can enter only with one of the official guides at the Forestry Department Visitor Centre, at the start of the trail. The Millet Forest Trail is a fairly strenuous 2.8-km (1¾-mile) walk that gives some lovely views down to the dam; guides will help identify all the birdlife. The turn-off to Millet is signposted from the west-coast highway just south of Marigot Bay.

ⓐ Forestry Department Visitor Centre ❶ 451 1691 ❶ Tour charge

St Lucia Distillers Rum Factory

Past the Marigot turn-off, the main road loops down through the Roseau banana plantation, the valley floor framed attractively by the interior hills. Before bananas became the main cash crop, the valley's flat, fertile plains were deemed ideal for the cultivation of sugar cane, much of which was processed at what's now the St Lucia Distillers Rum Factory. Though it's still a working factory, producing the local Admiral Rodney, Chairman's Reserve and Bounty rums, you can take a look around the facility via the Rhythm of Rum tour, in which the distilling process is entertainingly explained stage-by-stage. You're also taken through a room exhibiting local Carnival costumes, and shown a video about rum production. At the end, there's the opportunity to taste each and every one of the 23 rums and liqueurs produced here, and buy them at discounted rates from the factory shop.

ⓐ Roseau Valley ❶ 456 3149 ⓦ www.saintluciarums.com ❶ 09.00–15.30 Mon–Fri, closed Sat & Sun ❶ Admission charge

TAKING A BREAK

Chateau Mygo House of Seafood ££ Relaxed, inexpensive place right on the water, on the nearside of the bay, so there's no need to take a water-taxi. The menu fuses seafood with Indian cooking – try the excellent fish *roti* – and there are also thin-crust pizzas, including one topped with lobster plush sushi and sashimi. The permanent two-for-one happy hour means it's also a great place to sink a few rum punches. Live music on Tuesday and Thursday evenings. ⓐ Marigot Bay ❶ 451 4772 Ⓦ www.chateaumygo.com ⓛ 07.00–23.00 daily

Doolittle's ££ Beachside restaurant of the Marigot Beach Club hotel, with a wide-ranging menu: burgers, soups, salads and sandwiches (try the flying fish) at lunchtime and a more ambitious dinner menu, including St Lucian pepper-pot stew, steaks and plenty of seafood, from Goan-style king prawns to Creole conch. There are different themes each night, from fish and chips (Wed) to barbecue (Sat). There's also a daily happy hour from 17.00 to 19.00, with a two-for-one cocktail each day. ⓐ Marigot Beach ❶ 451 4974 Ⓦ www.marigotbeachclub.com ⓛ 12.00–22.00 daily

AFTER DARK

Rainforest Hideaway £££ A fantastic location on a deck right over the water on the far side of the bay, with a backdrop of mangrove, lovely views over to the marina and underwater lights illuminating the passing shoals of fish. The sophisticated menu includes such delights as lamb rack stuffed with mushroom and goat's cheese, or jerk shrimp and scallops with Parmesan risotto and a lime ginger cream, and the two-course set menu takes the price down. It's a very atmospheric place for a drink, too, with an excellent wine list. ⓐ Marigot Bay ❶ 451 4485 Ⓦ www.rainforesthideawaystlucia.com ⓛ 12.00–15.00, 18.00–22.00 Mon & Wed–Sat, 12.00–22.00 Sun, closed Tues ❶ Book ahead

◔ *Anse La Raye is a pretty fishing village*

Anse La Raye

South of Roseau Valley, the coast road climbs and dips over the hilly terrain before descending into Anse La Raye, one of the west's main fishing villages, and the scene of the island's most popular fish fry (see page 52). Very much off the tourist trail other than during this Friday night event, it's a quiet place of shabbily picturesque, weather-beaten wooden homes and small shops, networked by a grid of narrow little streets. Many of the buildings are more than a hundred years old, and are very photogenic examples of English and French colonial architecture. Around town, there are a few things to see and do, from the relics at La Sikwi Sugar Mill to swimming at the gorgeous beach and the River Rock Waterfall.

BEACHES

Though you'll see locals taking a dip, and the calm, clear waters are certainly quite inviting, **Anse La Raye** is very much a fishing beach rather than a place to spread out a towel and settle in for a day soaking up the sun – as demonstrated by the smart new jetty and fishing complex courtesy of the Japanese government.

Reachable via Ti Kaye Village resort (see page 109), and also visited by boat cruises and water-taxis from Soufrière, **Anse Cochon** is a far better bet for a day on the beach. A gorgeous sweep of white and brown sand backed by trees, with clear, calm waters, it's one of the prettiest beaches on the west coast. The bay floor holds the hulk of the *Lesleen M*, one of St Lucia's best wreck dives, and there are some great dive sites nearby – the offshore reefs offer some excellent snorkelling as well. Gear rental, guided dives and certification packages are available from Island Dive, based at Ti Kaye Village resort.

Island Dive ⓐ Ti Kaye Village ⓣ 456 8110 ⓦ www.islanddiversstlucia.com ⓔ diving@tikaye.com ⓘ Pre-booking recommended

◆ *La Sikwi Sugar Mill, Anse La Raye*

THINGS TO SEE & DO

Canaries

A pretty little fishing village nestled at the base of high hills, Canaries is best seen from above, with a viewpoint to the south of the village affording a panoramic view over its labyrinth of streets and picturesque white-sand bay, home to a fleet of colourful fishing boats.

La Sikwi Sugar Mill

A short drive inland from Anse La Raye, La Sikwi is a beautifully restored old sugar mill surrounded by landscaped gardens thick with tropical trees and flowers. Originally built in 1860, when sugar was the island's main crop (*sikwi* means 'sugar' in Creole), the estate later switched to producing cocoa, vegetables and fruits including limes: the latter were processed here and exported as lime oil and juice. The cut-stone main building holds the estate's huge old waterwheel, as well as equipment for juicing limes and boiling cane juice, and guides explain a little about the sugar industry and the estate's history. You also take a short walk around the grounds, and finish up at the bar area. It's an extremely pretty place, but can be hard to find; most people visit as part of an organised tour, so it's not well signposted. Driving south along the main street through Anse La Raye, take the left-hand turning opposite the phone booth. The road forks almost straightaway; take the right-hand route, passing the village school. La Sikwi is on the right; cross the bridge over the stream and follow the path to the main building.

ⓐ Anse La Raye ✆ 451 0425 🕒 08.00–16.00 daily ❶ Admission charge

River Rock Waterfall

As you enter Anse La Raye from the north, a painted sign advertises River Rock Falls, reachable via a short footpath. Surrounded by greenery and with a pool for swimming, the 4.5-m (15-ft) cascade is overlooked by a changing area, and a bar selling beers and soft drinks.

ⓐ Anse La Raye 🕒 No set hours ❶ Admission charge

ANSE LA RAYE FISH FRY

Each Friday from around 19.00, Anse La Raye's ocean-side Front Street is the scene of this brilliant culinary extravaganza, with traffic blocked off, music booming from speakers and a host of stalls selling fresh fish and seafood (lobster and conch as well as a wide variety of fish) and local specialities such as accra fritters and floats, which are made with black-eyed peas; you eat at little tables on the street or on the sand. The rum flows freely and it's a hugely friendly and fun experience, with the party usually continuing until the wee hours.

TAKING A BREAK

Ti Manje £ In-resort bar and grill on a deck right on the beach, open to non-guests. Baguettes, burgers and salads are served all day, and there's a daily happy hour from 16.30 to 17.30. 🅐 Ti Kaye Village Resort, Anse Cochon 🏵 456 8101 🅦 www.tikaye.com 🕒 08.00–22.30 (last food order 16.30) daily

Kai Manje ££ Set on an open veranda overlooking Anse Cochon Beach, this resort restaurant serves soups, salads and sandwiches for lunch, alongside more substantial dinner fare such as jerk chicken or fresh fish; there's a good wine list, too. Service is excellent and the setting is very romantic. 🅐 Ti Kaye Village Resort, Anse Cochon 🏵 456 8101 🅦 www.tikaye.com 🕒 12.00–15.00, 19.00–22.30 (last orders 21.00) daily

Soufrière

The island's main tourist centre after Rodney Bay, Soufrière is a very different kettle of fish. Rather than glitzy bars and hulking hotels, this is much more refined and charming, with a cluster of exclusive places to stay and eat capitalising on the stunning backdrop provided by the Pitons, and a host of attractions around town that make the most of the area's volcanic geology, from hot mineral springs to lush botanic gardens. Soufrière took a battering from Hurricane Tomas in 2010, with flooding in the town and landslides in the surrounding areas, but the clean-up was swift and today there's little trace of the damage.

BEACHES

North of Soufrière, a terribly potholed but drivable coast road leads to **Anse Chastanet**, one of the best beaches in the area, with fine brown sand dotted with the thatched shelters (for use of guests of the Anse Chastanet and Jade Mountain resorts), and a wonderful reef close to the shore with some of St Lucia's best snorkelling: huge brain corals and lively, colourful fish. **Scuba St Lucia** dive shop, right on the beach, rents gear and offers PADI certification, guided dives and snorkelling trips. Further north along the same road, **Anse Mamin** is a smaller and less busy beach. On the other side of town, **Anse des Pitons** is spectacularly located right between the two Pitons. It's also the site of the plush Jalousie Plantation hotel, which imported the gleaming white sand, but non-guests are free to swim here; the combination of clear green waters, teeming reefs and the imposing bulk of the Pitons is absolutely magnificent, as is the snorkelling and diving – the bay is part of St Lucia's **National Marine Park**. The hotel's dive shop also rents gear and offers guided dives and snorkelling trips. Note that you can take water-taxis to all these beaches from Soufrière waterfront.

Scuba St Lucia @ Anse Chastanet ☏ 465 8242 Ⓦ www.scubastlucia.com
Dive Jalousie @ Anse des Pitons ☏ 459 7666 Ⓦ www.thejalousie plantation.com Ⓔ reservations@thejalousieplantation.com

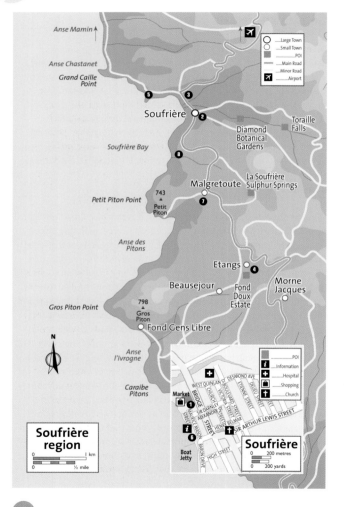

Anse Mamin

Anse Chastanet

Grand Caille Point

5

3

Soufrière ○ 2

Toraille Falls

Diamond Botanical Gardens

Soufrière Bay

8

La Soufrière Sulphur Springs

Malgretoute

743 ▲ Petit Piton

7

Petit Piton Point

Anse des Pitons

Etangs ○ 4

Morne Jacques

Beausejour ○

Fond Doux Estate

Gros Piton Point

798 ▲ Gros Piton

○ Fond Gens Libre

N

Anse l'Ivrogne

Caraibe Pitons

Soufrière region
0 — 1 km
0 — ½ mile

○ .....Large Town
○ .....Small Town
■ .....POI
— .....Main Road
— .....Minor Road
✈ .....Airport

WEST QUINLAN ST   DESMOND AVE
Market ■   1
BRIDGE STREET
SIR DARNLEY STREET
CHURCH STREET
MAURICE MASON STREET
ALEXANDER STREET
VICTORIA STREET
ETIENNE STREET
DRUDE STREET
HENRY BELMAR
SIR ARTHUR LEWIS STREET
i   6
BARON DRIVE
HIGH STREET

Boat Jetty

■ .....POI
i .....Information
✚ .....Hospital
🛍 .....Shopping
✝ .....Church

Soufrière
0 — 200 metres
0 — 200 yards

THINGS TO SEE & DO

Diamond Botanical Gardens

Set in the lush surrounds of the Soufrière Estate, a former sugar-cane and citrus plantation occupying the valley inland of the town, the Diamond Botanical Gardens has trails through beautifully landscaped tropical gardens thick with exotic plants and flowers, as well as the Diamond Waterfall, a 10-m (33-ft) cascade that splashes over rocks coloured by the sulphuric waters. You can't swim in the falls' pool, but it's well worth taking a soak in the adjacent thermal baths, originally developed by Louis XIV for his troops, and said to have been used by Napoleon's wife, Josephine. Today, you wallow in the warm waters in tiled modern cubicles or an outdoor pool.

ⓐ Soufrière Estate ① 459 7565 ⓦ www.diamondstlucia.com
🕙 10.00–17.00 Mon–Sat, 10.00–15.00 Sun ❗ Admission charge, plus charge to use the baths/pool

Fond Doux Estate

Signposted from the coast road just south of Soufrière, Fond Doux is a 54.6-ha (135-acre) working cocoa plantation (95 per cent of the crop is exported to Hershey's Chocolate manufacturers), first established in the 19th century, which now encompasses a hotel, restaurant and tour site. Its collection of beautifully restored colonial-era wooden buildings include the wonderfully rickety cocoa-drying shed, with extendable trays that allow the beans to mature in the sunlight.

In addition, there are three trails that you can walk, accompanied by guides who can tell you all about the plants and flowers and provide some local history. The Estate Trail is a gentle trek through the grounds surrounding the main buildings, planted with cocoa, bananas and coconuts as well as a host of flowers, while the East Ruins Trail takes you to the remains of a French-built fortification. The Chateaubelair Trail is more strenuous, following an old Maroon (escaped slave) route. It climbs up to the estate's highest point, which provides lovely views back to the Pitons.

@ South of Soufrière off west-coast highway ☏ 459 7545 ⓦ www.fond
douxestate.com ⏰ 08.00–17.00 daily ❶ Admission charge for guided tour

The Pitons

St Lucia's iconic landmarks, these much-photographed twin volcanic
peaks are easily the island's most stunning physical feature, and are the
result of eruptions some 30–40 million years ago. Distinctively conical in
shape, shrouded with greenery and rising right up from the sea, the
Pitons dominate the area and are visible from all over the south of
the island. The larger, though not by much, is Gros Piton, looming
797 m (2,615 ft) over the village of Choiseul, while some 5 km (3 miles)
to the north and overlooking Soufrière town, Petit Piton rises to
743 m (2,438 ft). It's possible to climb both peaks, but the near-vertical
Petit Piton is rarely attempted, and in any case its slopes harbour fragile
ecosystems. If you want to tackle the gentler Gros Piton (a four-hour
round trip), contact Heritage Tours, which offers guided hikes from Fond
Gens Libre village. Some of the best views of the Pitons are from the
two lookout points on the main road to the north of Soufrière town,
where vendors set up to sell crafts and tout for tips.
Heritage Tours @ La Clery, Castries ☏ 458 1454 ⓦ www.heritagetours
stlucia.org

La Soufrière Sulphur Springs

Much touted as a drive-in volcano, in that the access road leads through
the 'crater' of what's now a collapsed volcano, La Soufrière is nonetheless
a fascinating place to visit. From the entrance booth, you head to the
smart new Interpretation Centre to watch a video on the geology of the
area and take a look at a small museum that centres on attempts to
exploit the volcano's geothermal power. Guides then walk you to the
edge of the active part of the volcano, a moonscape of craters, grey rocks
and bubbling pools of mud emitting clouds of sulphurous steam that
hangs heavily – and pungently – in the air. La Soufrière last erupted in
1766, and there's little danger of another blow anytime soon, but as the
water and mud come to the surface at 70–90°C (158–194°F), you'll be

🔺 *Bubbling mud and steam at La Soufrière Sulphur Springs*

◆ *Soufrière town in the shadow of the magnificent Piton mountains*

thankful for the distance provided by the boundary fence. You can also take a dip in a thermal pool and anoint yourself with volcanic mud, said to be therapeutic.

ⓐ Off west-coast highway, south of Soufrière ⓣ 459 7686
ⓛ 09.00–17.00 daily ⓘ Admission charge

Soufrière town
Overlooked to the south by the towering bulk of Petit Piton, and nestled at the foot of a fertile volcanic valley, Soufrière is a unique place, bubbling with a slow-paced energy and well worth exploring on foot (its narrow streets and unsigned one-way system mean driving is inadvisable in any case). Spreading back from a brown-sand beach, its collection of fine colonial-era buildings, with their second-floor verandas and intricate gingerbread fretwork, are interspersed with newer concrete structures built after successive fires and hurricanes put paid to the original townscape. The grassy square at the centre of town, just in from the waterfront, is bordered by several lovely old buildings, as well as the pretty Lady of Assumption church, while down by the sea a walkway runs parallel to the sand, dotted with benches. Across from the boat jetty, the tourist office provides local information.
Soufrière Tourist Office ⓐ Soufrière Waterfront ⓣ 459 7419
ⓛ 08.00–16.00 Mon–Fri, 08.00–12.00 Sat, closed Sun

Toraille Falls
A little further on along the road from the Diamond Gardens, Toraille is a smaller and much quieter complex of landscaped gardens set around a pretty 15-m (50-ft)-high waterfall, overhung by foliage and with a deep pool at its base that you can swim in; there are changing facilities on-site. Short walkways thread through the gardens, which harbour a pretty array of tropical flowers and plants – look out for distinctive green gourds of the calabash tree, hollowed out by locals and sold on craft stalls. Toraille suffered extensive damage in Hurricane Tomas, but has since been refurbished and is set to re-open fully in September 2011.
ⓐ Fond St Jacques ⓣ No phone ⓛ 09.00–17.00 daily ⓘ Admission charge

TAKING A BREAK

Archie's Creole Pot £ ❶   The most sociable of several basic locals' places along this street, serving simple St Lucian fare such as Creole fish with rice and salad, as well as *rotis* and hearty soups. Also good for a drink and mingling with the locals. ⓐ 9 Bridge St, Soufrière ❶ 459 7760 ⓛ 08.00–late daily

Gee's Bon Manje ££ ❷   Set in an open-sided wood cabin just off the main road, this popular spot is a good bet both for dining and hanging out by the bar, serving reasonably priced local food and offering board games for drinkers and diners, too. ⓐ La Pearl Estate, Soufrière ❶ 457 1418 ⓛ 07.00–23.00 daily

La Haut Plantation ££ ❸   With fabulous views over Soufrière to the Pitons, this is a relaxed place for lunch, serving a delicious and inexpensive three-course set menu of Creole food (soup, fish or chicken, and a simple dessert) on the breezy veranda. À la carte is also available, from dorado with lime ginger sauce to pastas – and the natural juices (especially the tamarind) are excellent. ⓐ West-coast highway north of Soufrière ❶ 459 7008 ⓦ www.lahaut.com ⓛ 08.00–21.00 daily

Jardin Cacao ££ ❹   A gorgeous semi-open-air setting surrounded by tropical flowers and foliage, and a tasty selection of local-style dishes such as seasoned sautéed conch or fresh fish, as well as lighter fare including sandwiches and salads. ⓐ Fond Doux Estate, south of Soufrière on the west-coast highway ❶ 459 7595 ⓦ www.fonddouxestate.com ⓛ 11.00–16.00, 18.00–20.00 daily

Lifeline Bar and Restaurant ££ ❺   With a nice location right on the beach, just a short walk from Soufrière on the Anse Chastanet road, this is a good choice for an inexpensive Creole breakfast, lunch and dinner (the seafood, from fish to conch and lobster, is especially tasty), as well as for drinks at the lovely bar, which is a popular sunset spot. There is live

⏏ *Diamond Botanical Gardens (see page 55)*

◆ *Anse des Pitons Beach, near Soufrière*

music every Wednesday night. ⓐ Hummingbird Beach Resort, Anse Chastanet Road, Soufrière ⓣ 459 7232 ⓛ 07.00–23.00 daily

La Petit Peak ££ ⑥ Tourist-oriented place in a breezy setting right on the Soufrière waterfront, popular with parties from boat cruises and offering an international-style menu of burgers, wraps and salads plus local fare such as *rotis*. ⓐ 2 Bay Street, Soufrière ⓣ 459 7838 ⓛ 08.00–23.00 Tues–Sun, closed Mon

Dasheene ££–£££ ⑦ With a fantastic setting in between and overlooking the Pitons, this in-hotel place at Ladera resort is one of St Lucia's best restaurants. Enjoy delicious Caribbean food with a sophisticated twist, from lamb curry with coconut risotto to vegetable tamales or 'catch of the day' in jerk butter. Puddings are delectable, and the Tcholit Bar is great for a sunset drink, too. The pool-bar menu is a less expensive alternative to the main restaurant, and there's an excellent Sunday brunch here as well. ⓐ West-coast highway, opposite La Soufrière Sulphur Springs ⓣ 459 6617 ⓦ www.ladera.com ⓛ 11.30–14.30 & 18.30–21.30 daily

Mango Tree £££ ⑧ With tables on an open-sided veranda in the shadow of Petit Piton, this place offers an eclectic selection of dishes, from seafood pasta to calamari or vegetarian and vegan fare made with vegetables grown organically on site. There's a Creole night on Thursday evenings, with jerk chicken and barbecued ribs, plus live music from a local band, and other dinner themes throughout the week. ⓐ Stonefield Estate Villas, off the west-coast highway south of Soufrière ⓣ 459 7037 ⓦ www.stonefieldvillas.com ⓛ 07.30–22.00 daily

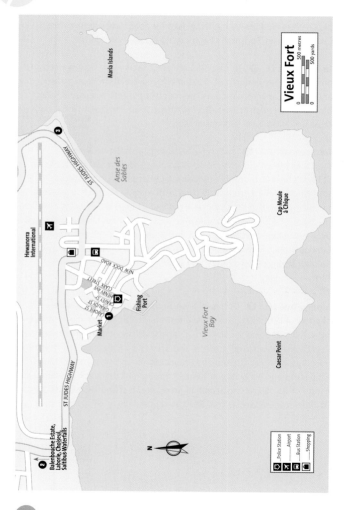

Vieux Fort

Maria Islands

Anse des Sablos

Cap Moule à Chique

Hewanorra International

Balenbouche Estate, Laborie, Choiseul, Saltibus Waterfalls

ST JUDES HIGHWAY

NEW DOCK ROAD

Market

ARBORT ST

GIRAUD ST

GRAVES ST

HENRY AVE

CLARK STREET

Fishing Port

Vieux Fort Bay

Caesar Point

Police Station
Airport
Bus Station
Shopping

0   500 metres
0   500 yards

N

Vieux Fort

The largest town in the south of the island, workaday Vieux Fort doesn't have a lot to offer visitors other than a flavour of St Lucia away from the resorts, but there is plenty to see and do in the surrounding area, from the spectacular Anse des Sables Beach to Balenbouche, a former plantation turned eco-conscious hotel and tour site.

BEACHES

One of the island's best beaches, **Anse des Sables** is a gorgeous 2-km (1¼-mile) sweep of fine white sand that stretches north from Cap Moule à Chique, with the Maria Islands rising out of the waters just offshore at the Vieux Fort end. Whipped by Atlantic winds that keep things nice and cool, the beach is St Lucia's windsurfing and kite-boarding hotspot, with enthusiasts taking to the water most weekends. You can rent gear and arrange lessons from **The Reef**, right on the beach (No 3 on the map), which also sells snacks and drinks.

Just north of Choiseul village, **Sab Wee-Sha Beach Park** offers a black-sand beach with good swimming, and a grassy area shaded by palm trees which makes a nice chill-out spot and is popular with locals.

The Reef ❷ Anse des Sables Beach ☏ 354 3418

THINGS TO SEE & DO

Balenbouche Estate

One of St Lucia's more interesting plantations turned tourist attraction, Balenbouche is a former sugar estate that's now privately owned and operated as an eco-lodge and tour site. You can drop by and walk around independently during opening hours, but it's best to call ahead and arrange a guided tour, conducted by one of the owners, which provides interesting background on the estate's colourful history. A site of Amerindian settlement, Balenbouche also passed through the hands of various European owners who planted everything from sugar, coconuts

◐ *The idyllic shoreline at Laborie Beach*

and limes to tobacco and vegetables, and who constructed the waterwheel and sugar factory, now both defunct. Trails through the property lead down to the Balenbouche River and to the sea.

ⓐ West-coast highway northwest of Vieux Fort ⓣ 455 1244 ⓦ www.balenbouche.com ⓛ 09.00–17.00 daily ⓘ Tour fee

Cap Moule à Chique

Towering over Vieux Fort and capping the southern end of the bay, with its busy container port, this grassy promontory offers some spectacular views over the southern coast, with the Maria Islands and Anse de Sables in the foreground; on a clear day, you can also make out St Vincent. Looking inland, the Pitons preside over the jagged, greenery-swathed hills. The road to the lighthouse on the further of the two hills is closed to the public, but a switchbacking tarmac road leads up to the communications towers for the best outlook in both directions.

Choiseul

A pretty little village with a smart white-and-blue-painted Catholic church overlooking a yellow-sand fishing beach, Choiseul is best known as the island's main centre for St Lucian craft items. Artisans from the village and the surrounding area sell their beautiful pieces at the Choiseul Arts and Crafts Development Centre, on the main coast road east of town. You'll find everything from bamboo cups and vases to dolls, basketry, pottery and mats, or hangings intricately woven from couscous grass.

Choiseul Arts and Crafts Development Centre ⓐ La Fargue ⓣ 459 3226 ⓛ 08.30–17.00 Mon–Sat, closed Sun

Laborie

A pretty, somnolent fishing village built around a palm-fringed white-sand beach lapped by calm, clear waters, Laborie is the sort of place where you'd expect to find a rash of hotels and restaurants – and, indeed, a huge Ritz Carlton resort has long been slated for construction on the outskirts of the village. The project has run into financial troubles, however, and for now, this is primarily the territory of the village's fishermen, whose fleet of

⬥ *River Doree Anglican Church, near Choiseul*

brightly painted wooden pirogues bob in the waters to the eastern side of the bay. To the western side, the **Rudy John Beach Park** has a couple of picnic tables, and the lack of boats here means this is the best place to swim. Tiny locals' bars in the village provide refreshments, and there are sometimes vendors selling soft drinks and snacks at the recreation area.
ⓐ West-coast highway northwest of Vieux Fort

Maria Islands

Just off the coast on the eastern side of Cap Moule à Chique, the uninhabited twin islets that make up the Maria Islands are home to a fascinating array of bird and plant life. An important breeding ground for gulls, boobies and the distinctive frigatebird, with its fork-shaped tail feathers, the dry, cactus-strewn islands are also home to the rare kouwes snake and to the whip-tail or ground lizard, found nowhere else in St Lucia and with a distinctive yellow, green and bright blue colouring. During the bird nesting season (May–August), both **Maria Major** 9.7 ha (24 acres) and **Maria Minor** 1.6 ha (4 acres) are off limits, but for the rest of the year, the St Lucia National Trust can arrange guided visits. With a small slip of white-sand beach and a path up to its peak, Major is the more interesting of the two.
St Lucia National Trust ⓣ 452 5005 ⓦ www.slunatrust.org ⓘ Tour charge

Saltibus Waterfalls

A 20-minute drive inland of Balenbouche, the community of Saltibus is the starting point for the trail to Saltibus Waterfalls, a beautiful and completely undeveloped cascade surrounded by lush rainforest foliage and with a deep pool for swimming. The hike to the falls, along the bank of the Saltibus River, will take around an hour and a half, and is best done with a local guide.
Saltibus Tour Guide Association c/o Delia Isaac ⓣ 287 6438 ⓘ Guide charge

Vieux Fort town

St Lucia's biggest settlement after Castries, Vieux Fort stretches back from the sea in a grid of busy streets lined with shops and businesses.

● *Anse des Sables, Vieux Fort*

HURRICANE TOMAS

On Saturday, 30 October 2010, St Lucians should have been enjoying the celebrations of the national Creole festival, Jounen Kwéyòl; instead, they found themselves sitting out the ravages of Hurricane Tomas. A Category 1 storm, with maximum sustained winds of 145 to 150 km/h (90 to 95 miles/h) – and even higher gusts – Tomas 'swept through Saint Lucia leaving unprecedented devastation in its wake', according to the island's prime minister, Stephenson King. The winds were bad enough, but the real damage came from the excessive rainfall, which led to flooding and catastrophic landslides that washed away homes, cars and roads, with Soufrière and Vieux Fort particularly badly damaged. Eight people lost their lives, and telephone, power and water supplies were knocked out for days. In the wake of the disaster, however, St Lucians rallied to repair the damage: rehabilitation was remarkably swift, and there's little visible evidence of Tomas' destructive power today.

It's more a place to stock up on supplies than to sightsee. The modern concrete buildings don't hold much charm, though there are a few colonial-era structures along the main road, Clark Street, and the **Old Plantation Yard** restaurant (see below) makes for an excellent lunch stop-off when touring the south. On the outskirts of town, making the most of the unusually flat terrain hereabouts, Hewanorra International Airport is another hive of activity.

TAKING A BREAK

Old Plantation Yard £ ❶ Occupying the backyard of a historic old wooden building from 1890, bedecked with fishing paraphernalia and shaded by fruit trees, this atmospheric place offers truly authentic St Lucian cuisine, cooked in the open on traditional coal pots. Breakfasts such as saltfish or smoked herring are served with cocoa tea, while lunch is curried or baked chicken, stewed lamb or steamed, fried or Creole-style fish served with all the traditional trimmings. The seasonal juices – tamarind, sorrel, sour orange – are delicious, too. ❸ Commercial St, Vieux Fort ❶ 454 6040 ◷ 08.00–18.00 daily (and by appointment for dinner)

Debbie's Place ££ ❷ Set in the hills overlooking Laborie, with tables on a covered terrace, this is a brilliant spot for local cuisine, with fresh seafood and Creole-style chicken, lamb and pork served up with delicious side dishes such as breadfruit balls and creamed pumpkin. On Sundays, there's a lavish and popular lunchtime buffet. ❸ West-coast highway, Laborie ❶ 455 1625 ◷ 07.00–22.00 daily

The Reef ££ ❸ Right on the beach, with tables under sea-grape trees and inside, this is one of the few tourist-oriented places hereabouts, with a cool surfers' vibe and a tasty menu of fish, lobster, squid and conch cooked Creole style, as well as grilled meats and lighter fare such as stuffed crab backs, saltfish and bakes, burgers and pizza. Popular with locals and tourists, it's a nice spot after dark, too, with a lively bar, pool table and wireless Internet. ❸ Anse des Sables Beach ❶ 354 3418 ◷ 08.00–22.00 daily, closed Mon in low season

◉ *Explore the hidden corners of St Lucia*

 **EXCURSIONS**
Out & about

The northern tip

Characterised by its expansive upmarket resorts and equally palatial
private homes, the Cap Estate area makes up St Lucia's northwest tip
and has a very chi-chi feel, its tiny roads flanked by lush hedges of
bougainvillea and croton and with the smooth greens of the St Lucia
Country Club Golf Course adding to the pastoral feel. Signs advertising
new resort complexes or posh gated communities seem to spring up on
every corner; the largest of these developments is the enormous Raffles
resort, currently under construction immediately northeast of Cas en Bas
beach and taking up a huge tract of land that will encompass an

◆ *The St Lucia Golf Club, Cap Estate*

TRAVEL ARRANGEMENTS

Though potholed in places, the road along the west coast past the **St Lucia Country Club Golf Course** is easily drivable in a normal car. To get to the east-coast beaches, however, you'll need a 4WD vehicle or a sturdy pair of legs and plenty of stamina. The access routes are rough dirt tracks rutted with deep potholes, and there are some very steep stretches that mean you shouldn't attempt to go at all after heavy rains.

18-hole golf course designed by Jack Nicklaus. Construction has also meant that the formerly beautiful views from Pointe Hardy are now marred by concrete, and the whole of Cap Estate feels very much like a private enclave. Still, it makes for an interesting drive, if only to get a feel for St Lucia at its most exclusive, or seek out black-sand coves such as Smugglers Cove and Anse Becune. In the evening it's worth splashing out on dinner at the exclusive Le Sport or Cotton Bay hotels (see page 76).

THINGS TO SEE & DO

Cas en Bas

Despite the construction of the huge Raffles St Lucia complex overlooking the beach to the north, Cas en Bas is still a relatively untouched, gorgeous, wide swathe of yellow sand with calm and shallow waters protected by an offshore reef. It's one of the few beaches on the northeast coast that's safe for swimming, and there's a great beach bar for lunches and drinks, too. The only drawback is the terrible access road, deeply potholed and suitable for 4WD vehicles only. Trim's riding stables offer beach rides here that include swimming with your horse in the sea – an unforgettable experience. To get to the beach, take the turn-off from the Castries–Gros Islet highway opposite the Gros Islet turning.

Trim's National Riding Academy ⓐ Cas en Bas ⓣ 450 8273
ⓦ www.trimsnationalridingacademy.com ❗ Tour charge

Grande Anse

A rugged arc of sand whipped by Atlantic waves and with currents that make swimming dangerous, Grande Anse is a spectacular beach, completely undeveloped and backed by green hillsides studded with cacti and scrubby trees. It's the primary nesting site on the island for leatherback turtles, huge specimens that return to the beach of their birth to lay eggs under cover of night. A protected marine reserve since 1986, the beach is the site of a turtle watch during the laying season (March to August), and visitors can camp out to see the moving and fascinating spectacle for themselves. Trips are organised by **St Lucia Heritage Tours**; places are limited, however, so it's best to book ahead. Wear something warm, since it gets cold at night.

St Lucia Heritage Tours ⓐ La Clery, Castries ⓣ 458 1454
ⓦ www.heritagetoursstlucia.org

TAKING A BREAK

Piano Piano £££ With sleek modern décor and a sophisticated ambience, this slick in-hotel restaurant is a great option for a special night out. The international fusion menu features such delights as tomato, rocket and feta tart or grilled lobster, and the wine and cocktail list is excellent – as are the intricate desserts. There's live music on Fridays, Saturdays and Sundays and smart dress is required. ⓐ Cotton Bay Village, Cas en Bas, Cap Estate ⓣ 456 5700 ⓦ www.cottonbayvillage.com
ⓛ 19.00–23.00 Mon–Sat, closed Sun

Tao £££ This is one of the island's top restaurants, in an elegant and sophisticated setting overlooking the ocean, and offering delicious and healthy Asian fusion cuisine, including exemplary sushi and sashimi. Other highlights include the seafood bouillabaisse, as well as some great vegetarian dishes and tasting platters if you just can't decide. Booking ahead is essential, and men must wear shirts, trousers and covered shoes. ⓐ Le Sport Hotel, Cap Estate ⓣ 457 7800
ⓦ www.thebodyholiday.com ⓛ 19.00–22.30 daily

⬤ *From north to south, St Lucia has a stunning coastline*

The east coast

Licked by the Atlantic waves and with a jagged coastline that rises up into corrugated hills and valleys, St Lucia's rugged east has an undeveloped feel at present. Most visitors see it only through a taxi window as they speed from the airport to the north of the island along the relatively fast road that traverses the east coast and cuts inland at Fond d'Or to meet the west highway at Cul de Sac Valley. This is all set to change, however, as the 243-ha (600-acre) Le Paradis resort, marina and golf-club complex, under construction outside Praslin Bay, is the first of a slew of developments planned for the area, which look set to alter its remote feel forever. Though the rough waters make many of the beaches dangerous for swimming, there are a couple of interesting inland attractions: the peaceful Mamiku Gardens, and tours of the interior aboard ATV quad bikes.

THINGS TO SEE & DO

ATV Paradise Tours

Just north of the small fishing village of Micoud, and marked by large signs on the highway, Paradise Tours offer brilliant excursions through the Davies Estate aboard rugged two-person quad bikes, which provide a brilliant way to see the countryside. The three-hour tours wind through the estate, a working 404-ha (1,000-acre) plantation that produces tropical fruits and vegetables, and take in the waterwheel of a former sugar plantation as well as crossing the Fond River (swimming is allowed) and riding through a section of rainforest. Wear covered shoes and long trousers, and expect to get a little dirty. Note that all riders must be over 18 (though children of 14 and over can ride as passengers).
ⓐ Fond Estate, Micoud ❶ 455 3245 ⓦ www.atvstlucia.com ⓛ Daily
❶ Tour charge; advanced booking essential

Dennery

Travelling southeast from Castries via the inland road, Dennery is first of the string of fishing villages along the eastern coastline. It's best seen from

⏷ *See beautiful orchids at the Mamiku Gardens*

above, as the coast road gives a nice view of the village tumbling down the hillside to the calm, protected bay with a tiny islet at its north end, but if you're in the area at the weekend, it's well worth visiting for the Saturday night fish fry. Similar to the event at Anse La Raye (see page 52), though smaller in scale and with fewer tourists and more of a party feel, it's a friendly event held right on the beach, and is a great chance to sample some inexpensive and delicious seafood as well as have a dance on the sand.

Mamiku Gardens

Just inland of Praslin Bay, and well signposted from the coast road, Mamiku is the largest of St Lucia's gardens, and one of the prettiest. Ranged up a hillside topped by a pretty colonial-era wooden house, the gardens are networked by paths that take you through formally planted areas thick with flowering plants and unusual trees as well as wilder areas of forest. Some specimens are labelled, while a printed guide, which you can pick up at the entrance, should enable you to identify some of the others. The orchids just below the main house are particularly spectacular and well worth a look. Benches overlook the lawns and snacks and drinks are available from the Brigand's Bar in the house, so named for the British battalions that were stationed here during battles with freed slaves known as brigands.

ⓐ East-coast highway ⓣ 455 3729 ⓛ 09.00–17.00 daily
❶ Admission charge

TAKING A BREAK

Fox Grove Inn ££ One of the island's best places for lunch or dinner, with lovely views over the inland banana plantations. Inexpensive yet sophisticated, the menu includes everything from lobster bisque to smoked kingfish salad, flying fish with aioli, and duck with pink pepper sauce; the Andalusian *zazuela* (fish and shellfish in a brandy and tomato sauce) is particularly delicious. ⓐ Mon Repos, just off the east-coast highway ⓣ 455 3271 ⓦ www.foxgroveinn.com ⓛ 08.00–10.00, 12.30–14.30, 19.00–22.00 daily

The interior

An immensely lush patchwork of hills and valleys covered with a thick growth of forest and interspersed with pretty rural villages, St Lucia's interior is spectacularly beautiful. There are some tiny roads that head towards the centre of the island and provide an easy-access view of the interior, but by far the best way to see it is to walk one of the many hiking trails maintained by the Forestry Department. The most accessible of the hikes are described here, but for details of more challenging treks, check the Forestry Department website. You can

● *The hills of the interior seen from Cul de Sac Valley*

The interior
0 — 2 km
0 — 1 mile

TAKE A HIKE!

St Lucia's hiking trails are maintained by the government's **Forestry Department**, which operates Ranger Stations at trailheads where you pay the (minimal) entrance fee, and can hire a guide if you choose. The trails covered here can be walked independently, though a Forestry Department guide can provide interesting commentary about the local fauna and flora. You can also go hiking with private tour companies such as **SunLink** or **St Lucia Heritage Tours**.

Forestry Department ⓐ Union Agricultural Station ⓣ 468 5649

St Lucia Heritage Tours ⓐ La Clery, Castries ⓣ 458 1454
ⓦ www.heritagetoursstlucia.org

SunLink Tours ⓐ Reduit Beach Avenue, Rodney Bay ⓣ 456 9100
ⓦ www.sunlinktours.com

also see the rainforest without exerting yourself by way of the rainforest aerial tram, with open gondolas providing fabulous forest views (see page 85).

THINGS TO SEE & DO

Barre de L'Isle Trail

Leading off from the main road that cuts across the centre of the island between Castries and Dennery, this is an easy 1.6-km (1-mile) trail that cuts into the main ridge dividing the east of the island from the west. At the trailhead, there's a hut where you can hire a guide, though the path is easy to follow independently: to return, you just double back on yourself. Though the forest blocks out views for the most part, there are some nice vistas of Mount Gimie, the island's highest peak at 950 m (3,117 ft), as well as the banana plantations of Cul de Sac valley and the east and west coastlines.

⏏ *Up, up and away at Rainforest Adventures, Babonneau*

Visitor centre ❷ Castries–Dennery road ☎ 453 3242 🕐 08.00–14.00 Mon–Fri, closed Sat & Sun ❶ Admission charge

Des Cartiers Rainforest Trail

One of the gentlest rainforest trails, this relatively flat 4-km (2½-mile) circular route takes you through some lovely pristine rainforest. There are two lookout points affording lovely views of the east coast (the entire trail is 300 m/984 ft above sea level), and you've a good chance of seeing Jacquot parrots, which favour the trees around the lookouts. To get to the trailhead and ranger station, take the signposted inland road from the east-coast highway just north of Micoud, from where it's a 20-minute drive.

Visitor centre ❸ Mahaut ☎ 454 5589 🕐 08.00–14.00 Mon–Fri, closed Sat & Sun ❶ Admission charge

Rainforest Adventures

Past Union, the Babonneau road twists through a string of pretty settlements to reach one of the island's most exciting attractions. Ranging up the forested slopes of the La Soucière mountain, Rainforest Adventures Complex offers the chance to ride on the open gondolas of the aerial tram, which glide silently above the rainforest floor, opening up spectacular views over the interior and down to the coast. From 40 m (130 ft) up, you get a bird's-eye view of the forest canopy, a thick network of gommier, châtaigne, ficus and magnolia trees interspersed with towering tree ferns and smothered with vines, orchids and bromeliads. Guides accompany you on the gondola and provide interesting and entertaining information on the fauna and flora.

You can also opt to get down for a short hike up to the first of ten 'tranopy' traverses, ziplines of up to 102 m (335 ft) long strung through the forest between platforms in the trees – exhilarating and unique. There are also hiking trails through the reserve, and birdwatching walks are conducted on Tuesdays and Saturdays. There's a gift shop and café situated at the base of the gondolas. You should wear trainers (or similar) and long trousers.

● *Looking towards the interior from Roseau Valley*

ⓐ Fond Asseau, signposted from the Babonneau road ⓣ 458 5151 for bookings ⓦ www.rainforestrams.com ⓛ 08.00–15.00 Tues–Fri & Sun, closed Sat & Mon (May–Sept) ⓘ Admission charge; booking essential

Union Agricultural Station and Union Trail

A short drive inland from the Castries–Gros Islet Highway along the Babonneau turn-off from the roundabout just north of town, this is the field headquarters of St Lucia's forestry division, and the site of a rather desultory mini-zoo where tiny cages hold orange-winged parrots, tortoises, agoutis, green monkeys and a couple of St Lucia's enormous iguanas, as well as the Jacquot parrot, endemic to St Lucia and the island's national bird. The site is also the starting point for the short Union Nature trail, a gentle amble into the surrounding forest. Guides can provide tours, or you can walk alone.

ⓐ Allan Bousquet Highway, signposted for Babonneau ⓣ 468 5645 ⓛ 08.00–16.30 daily ⓘ Admission charge

Island-hopping from St Lucia

With its plum position in the middle of the Lesser Antilles chain, St Lucia is ideally placed for island-hopping. The closest destination is **Martinique**. This chic French island boasts gorgeous white-sand beaches, thick interior rainforest and plenty of Gallic charm. It's quite feasible to pop over for the day from St Lucia to indulge in fresh baguettes, cheese and excellent wine. The day tour offered by **Wave Riders** (☎ 452 0808 🌐 www.stluciawaveriders.com) starts with a pickup at Rodney Bay Marina. Their fast catamaran zips over the waters to Martinique's handsome capital, Fort de France, where you can shop and sightsee or take an organised tour. You then head to Anse Noire Beach for lunch, snorkelling and swimming before cruising back to St Lucia.

You can reach Martinique, **Guadeloupe, Dominica, Îles des Saintes** and **Marie Galante** by way of the *L'Express des Îles* fast ferry service (☎ 456 5000 🌐 www.express-des-iles.com), which departs from the Port Authority terminal at Bananes Bay in Castries, on the west side of the harbour. Dominica is known as the 'nature island', as its rugged interior is covered with thick rainforest, laced with hiking trails. Butterfly-shaped Guadeloupe, meanwhile, is renowned for its excellent cuisine, great beaches and mountainous interior. Just to the south, Îles des Saintes and Marie Galante make for lovely side-trips.

St Vincent and the Grenadines, Barbados and the rest of the eastern Caribbean are also reachable by short plane journeys, departing from the George F L Charles Airport in Castries. The main operator is LIAT (☎ 1 268 480 5601 🌐 www.liat.com). With its black-sand beaches and undeveloped interior, rugged St Vincent is a complete contrast to the Grenadine Islands, with their white-sand beaches and fantastic snorkelling. Barbados is known as the Caribbean's 'Little England' and has some of the region's best beaches and an excellent tourist infrastructure.

▶ *Sailing boats at Marigot Bay*

 LIFESTYLE
The St Lucian way

LIFESTYLE

Food & drink

LOCAL FOOD

St Lucia's Creole cuisine is a delicious blend of African, French and Indian influences, making good use of the island's vast array of fresh produce. You'll often see fish, meat and shrimp dishes cooked in a Creole sauce, usually spicy and tomato-based.

The classic Creole accompaniment to any main dish is ground provisions, which are starchy and dense tubers such as yam, dasheen and cassava, boiled until tender and served as side dishes. Green bananas (known as figs) are sometimes on offer, too, as are slices of fried ripe plantain, the larger relative of the banana. You may also get breadfruit, a starchy and delicious fruit served baked, fried or as breadfruit balls. The Indian influence has given the island *roti*, a thin, flour-based bread wrapped around curried meat, vegetables or fish – these make a cheap, delicious and filling lunch.

In terms of fish and seafood, St Lucian menus feature staples such as red snapper and mahi-mahi or dorado (often also called dolphin, but a different species from the one Flipper belonged to!), both succulent white fish, as well as the denser, meatier kingfish and tuna. Seafood is predictably delicious, with shrimp and lobster cooked Creole-style, curried or with classic garlic butter. Squid and conch (locally known as *lambi*) are also available and well worth trying if you see them. Fish broth is a fortifying soup, though you'll more often see pepper-pot, a thick soup of beef and the spinach-like callaloo; or bouillabaisse, a tomato-based seafood concoction.

Meat-lovers are well served here, too, with local staples such as curried goat or chicken alongside steaks and lamb or pork dishes. For people on the go, vendors also cook up spicy and delicious jerk chicken on roadside barbecues.

The traditional St Lucian breakfast is saltfish and bakes: salted codfish cooked up with onion and cucumber, served with light and fluffy fried dumplings and accompanied by a steaming cup of chocolate tea, the nutmeg-laced local cocoa.

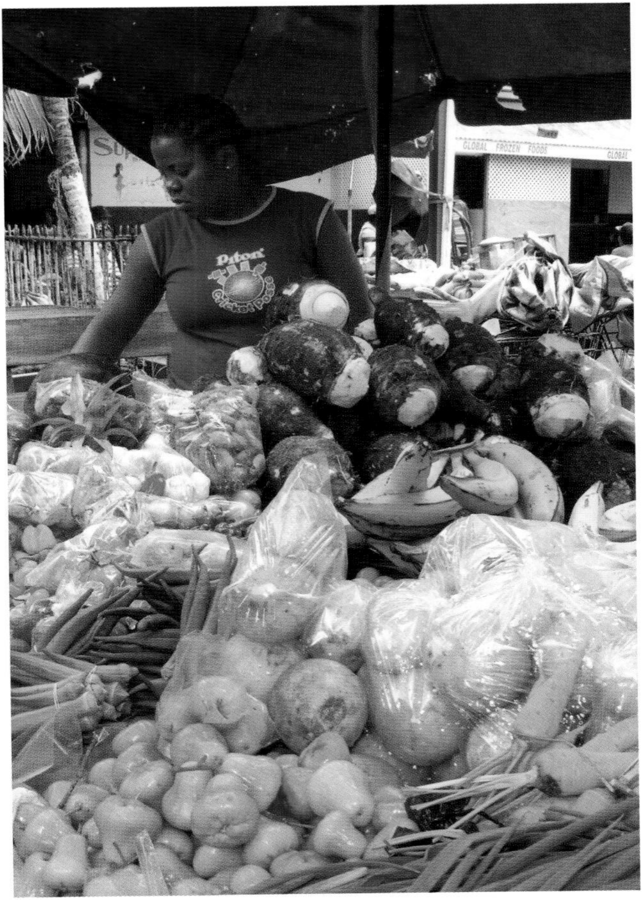

Fresh produce on sale at Castries market

DESSERTS & SWEETS

Desserts make good use of local fruits, with specialities including rum-smothered banana flambé and cheesecakes topped with guava or passion fruit. Locally produced ice cream is also delicious, and comes in a wide variety of flavours from coconut to rum and raisin or the delectable soursop. Banana bread and rich, dark fruitcake are also well worth seeking out. In terms of sweets, there are several sugary concoctions made with coconut, molasses and cane sugar to enjoy, usually sold at roadside stalls.

DRINKS

St Lucia's beer is Piton, a light and refreshing lager sold in almost every bar. You can also get bottled Heineken® and Guinness® in most places, and a host of international beers at tourist-oriented bars in the north. As for rum, the local brands include Bounty white rum, the staple of many a fruity cocktail, as well as the smoother and more expensive Chairman's Reserve and Admiral Rodney, both dark rums redolent with molasses. All the international brands of spirits are widely available, while restaurants and bars carry an increasingly good range of French and New World wines. Most bars mix up a mean rum punch, as well as tropical staples such as pina coladas, zombies, frozen daiquiris and the like; and in Rodney Bay there are a couple of bars producing some seriously sophisticated cocktails, too. Many bars have daily happy hours, during which you'll get two-for-one drinks or cocktails – ask around.

In terms of soft drinks, the usual array of fizzy products are available everywhere (though look out for the unusual Malta, a fortifying, effervescent malt drink). With a vast choice on offer, however, it's far better to ask for natural juice such as tart and refreshing tamarind or golden apple, as well as more familiar pineapple, passion fruit and guava blends. Mauby, made from boiled tree bark and something of an acquired taste, is sweet with a bitter aftertaste.

Another excellent choice is a coconut water, often sold from the back of a truck at the roadside; the vendor slices off the top for you to drink the water, then cuts the nut in half when you've finished so you can scoop out the nutritious jelly using a piece of the husk as a spoon. Bottled water is widely available; tap water is chlorinated and drinkable, but be aware that it may upset stomachs not used to it.

VEGETARIANS

Given the wide availability of seafood, vegetarians who eat fish will have no problems filling up. Otherwise, most restaurants will have a non-meat option, be it a vegetable *roti* or pasta dish, from simple tomato sauce to the delicious local macaroni pie. Pumpkin soup is a menu staple, and is usually made with vegetable stock (though do check, as pig tail is occasionally included for flavour), while peas (actually pulses such as green lentils or black-eyed peas) cooked up in sauce are usually served as an accompaniment to a meat or fish dish; you can always ask for a main-course portion instead.

RESTAURANTS

St Lucia has restaurants of every ilk, from fantastically upmarket gourmet establishments in gorgeous settings to simple diners doling out takeaway boxes of hearty Creole food to local workers. In between, the resorts have legions of places where you can sample local cuisine or have a burger, steak, pasta or some seafood at fairly reasonable prices. Many of them have lovely settings by the ocean, and are especially romantic at night, when fairy lights twinkle in the palm trees.

The island's fish fries, at Anse La Raye, Dennery and, to a lesser extent, Gros Islet, offer delicious seafood at reasonable prices, and have an unbeatable ambience, too. For something quick and convenient, though lacking the local feel, there are also international fast-food places throughout the island offering standard burger, chips and pizza meals.

Reservations are only necessary for the smartest restaurants and, in terms of dress codes, the most expensive places require men to wear a jacket, long trousers and covered shoes. Otherwise, casual clothes are fine. When it comes to tipping, you'll find that restaurants almost always add a 10 per cent service charge to the bill; if service is good, it's customary to leave 10–15 per cent on top of this.

Shopping

St Lucia has plenty of shopping opportunities, with two duty-free complexes, and crafts on sale island-wide at shops, stalls and the Castries market. For more everyday items, the **JQ Shopping Mall** and **Bay Walk Mall** in Rodney Bay each have a large supermarket as well as several clothing boutiques and shoe shops, and there's a smaller range of shops in **Gablewoods Mall** on the Castries–Gros Islet Highway. Castries itself isn't brilliant for shopping, but if you want to check out the stores you'll find the bulk along **William Peter Boulevard**.

In terms of prices, some rate St Lucia's craft items as a little more expensive than on neighbouring islands, but bear in mind that vendors are almost always up for a bit of bargaining, and you can make great savings at the duty-free stores.

As well as handicrafts, good gifts to take home include rum (the cheapest outlet is the **St Lucia Distillers** factory shop – see page 46), as well as local liqueurs made with everything from orange and coconut to peanuts. From the supermarkets, you can also pick up St Lucian nutmeg and cinnamon, and places such as **Fond Doux Estate** sell sticks of locally produced cocoa, aromatic with spices and completely delicious.

HANDICRAFTS

There is a huge array of locally made souvenirs available in St Lucia, and some are of very high quality. The main place to shop for crafts is the **Vendors' Arcade** in Castries, which sells everything from cheap and kitsch plastic key rings, placemats and the like to T-shirts, basketry and paintings. For something more specialised, **Caribelle Batik** on Morne Fortune have sarongs and dresses made on the spot; also on Morne Fortune, **Eudovik's Art Studio** has a fantastic selection of woodcarvings. Just south of Soufrière on the approach road to the Jalousie Plantation hotel, **Zaca Masks** produce unusual, brightly coloured masks with an African feel. For the best in local craft, however, head to **Choiseul** in the southeast (see page 67), where artisans produce some really gorgeous pottery and woven goods.

DUTY-FREE SHOPPING

On opposite sides of Castries Harbour, the **Pointe Seraphine** and **La Place Carenage** shopping centres hold a similar range of upmarket stores, icily air-conditioned and with racks of perfumes, designer watches, brand-name jewellery and the like at tax-free prices. Pointe Seraphine is adjacent to the cruise-ship dock and popular with passengers, while La Place Carenage is on the southern edge of the harbour. There are also duty-free outlets at **JQ Mall** and **Bay Walk Mall** in Rodney Bay, and the **Marina Village** in Marigot Bay.

Note that you must present your passport and outbound ticket in order to buy goods duty free.

🔺 *Take away a souvenir from Castries Central Market*

Children

St Lucia is a great destination for children. No vaccinations are needed, the water is safe to drink and there's endless fun to be had on the island's beaches, playing with sand and paddling or swimming in the warm, calm Caribbean Sea.

ATTITUDES TOWARDS CHILDREN

Most St Lucians love children and are very indulgent towards them, and travelling with children will ensure you meet and interact with many more locals than you would in an adults-only group. However, bear in mind that while children are cherished here, attitudes to parenting can seem quite old-fashioned compared to those in Europe or America. St Lucian children are taught to be respectful of adults at all times, and backchatting youngsters will certainly raise a few eyebrows, as will all-out tantrums.

It's also sensible to follow the locals' example and put small children in trunks or swimming costumes whenever they go in the water – St Lucian children don't tend to swim naked. You may also find that older St Lucians are quite free with their advice on the correct way to look after your child – such as covering babies' heads (despite the balmy temperatures), if they're out after dark.

SAFETY IN THE SUN

Bear in mind that the tropical sun is strong, and children – especially babies and toddlers – need special protection. It's a good idea to come prepared with beachwear that protects their heads and necks (such as hats with custom-designed flaps), to keep them in T-shirts while on the beach and, of course, to slather on the high-factor (50+) sunblock at all times, even when you're not at the beach. Tinted goggles can also be very useful for blocking out the glaring sun while swimming.

ATTRACTIONS FOR CHILDREN

Beaches

Younger children will find endless enjoyment in building sandcastles and playing in the water. Beach toys are available on the island, but the selection isn't fantastic so it's best to bring them from home. However, think twice before letting children use untethered lilos or other inflatables in the sea – drifting can happen very quickly, even in calm waters.

Boat trips

Boat trips (see page 98) can be brilliant fun, especially if you plump for the rigging-swathed *Liana's Ransom* 'pirate ship'. A day on this 42-m (140-ft) brig promises fun for all the family. Children can even get dressed up as pirates for the day.

Horse riding

This is an exciting option for older children. Trim's National Riding Academy (see page 75) offers riding lessons and has experienced tour guides.

Pigeon Island National Landmark

Older children might enjoy clambering around on the ruins here (see pages 40 and 42), while the grassy lawns shaded by trees are ideal for spreading out a blanket and letting babies and toddlers play outdoors.

Water park

Another idea is to buy a day-pass for the Coconut Bay all-inclusive hotel in Vieux Fort (see page 111), which has a brilliant water park with slides, a lazy river and fountains for swimming and splashing about in, as well as a well-equipped toddlers' club with its own water area.

EATING OUT

In tourist areas, children are welcomed in restaurants, many of which have children's menus, but you won't find local family parties dining out late as you would in, say, Spain or Italy, nor will you win over the staff if your kids run rampant or scatter their toys between the tables.

Sports & activities

St Lucia has a wealth of things to do on both water and land, including cruises along the coast to view the Pitons, big-game fishing, scuba diving, ATV bike rides and hiking. For a chance to unwind, you also have the option of some luxurious spas or a laid-back round of golf at St Lucia's public golf course.

BOAT TRIPS

One of the very best things to do in St Lucia, a cruise down the coastline provides a wonderful perspective of the island. Sunset tours are a romantic way to spend an evening, while day trips offer fun for the whole family. Most trips go down to the Pitons, and have stops for swimming and snorkelling. An open bar is usually included, as is lunch on a full-day trip. Some recommended tour operators include:

Carnival Party Cruises A number of catamaran cruises to choose from, including one specially designed for families. ☎ 452 5586
🌐 www.carnivalsailing.com

Endless Summer All-day and sunset catamaran cruises from the Rodney Bay area. ☎ 450 8651 🌐 www.stluciaboattours.com

Mystic Man Cruises Soufrière-based and offering more specialised trips such as whale-watching, fishing and eco-tours. ☎ 459 7783
🌐 www.mysticmantours.com

Sea Spray Catamaran cruises and trips aboard *Liana's Ransom*, a replica of an 18th-century gaffed schooner – the archetypal 'pirate' boat. Trips include a Pirate Family Adventure. ☎ 452 8644
🌐 www.seaspraycruises.com

FISHING

St Lucia's waters teem with big-game fish such as blue marlin, sailfish and tuna, and there are plenty of sports fishing boats available for day or half-day deep-sea fishing charters.

Captain Mike's ☎ 452 7044 🌐 www.captmikes.com

Hackshaws Charters ☎ 453 0553 🌐 www.hackshaws.com

🔺 *Keep your children safe if they take to the water for a boat trip*

◐ Ride the waves around St Lucia's stunning coastline

GOLF

St Lucia's public course, the **St Lucia Country Club Golf Course**, is located in a superb setting at the northern tip of the island, its fairways overlooking the Caribbean Sea. It has 18 holes and a clubhouse with restaurant and bar. Its facilities also include a driving range and practice putting green. ⓐ Cap Estate ⓣ 450 8523 ⓦ www.stluciagolf.com

HELICOPTER TOURS

This is an amazing way to see the island, and not as expensive as you might think. Options range from ten-minute trips around the north to a half-hour flight over the whole island. Covering the major sights, the tours include a lively commentary from your pilot. You can book directly or through your holiday rep. ⓐ George F L Charles Airport ⓣ 453 6950 ⓦ www.stluciahelicopters.com

HIKING

Covered in a thick tangle of rainforest, St Lucia's lush interior makes for some lovely hiking, and many of the best walks pass a waterfall where you can stop for a swim. Trails are shaded and range from easy to challenging. Some of the more accessible and undemanding routes are listed on pages 83–7.

JUNGLE TOURS

This fleet of open-topped jeeps offer fun off-road trips to waterfalls and far-flung beaches from hotels island-wide. ⓣ 715 3438 ⓦ www.jungletoursstlucia.com

SCUBA DIVING & SNORKELLING

St Lucia has some fantastic diving and snorkelling, with the reefs off the shore of Soufrière and the Pitons especially rich with sea life, and protected as part of the island's marine park. Notable dives include the Keyhole Pinnacles and the wreck of the *Lesleen M*, a freighter sunk in 1986 to act as an artificial reef and arguably one of the best dive sites in St Lucia. Rodney Bay also has some worthy sites, including La Roche and Dinosaur

Reef, while northern sites include Smugglers Cove and the coral gardens offshore of Le Sport hotel.

As well as getting PADI certification, you can participate on a resort dive, for which you receive on-the-spot training. Guided snorkelling trips are also available, as is gear rental. For more information about dive shops in the Soufrière area, see page 53.

Dive Fair Helen ⓐ Marigot Bay ⓣ 451 7716 ⓦ www.divefairhelen.com
Dive Jalousie ⓐ Anse des Pitons ⓣ 459 7666 ⓦ www.jalousie plantation.com
Frog's Diving ⓐ Rodney Bay Village ⓣ 458 0798 ⓦ www.frogs diving.com
Scuba St Lucia ⓐ Anse Chastanet ⓣ 459 7755 ⓦ www.scubastlucia.com
Scuba Steve's Diving ⓐ Rodney Bay ⓣ 450 9433 ⓦ www.scubasteves diving.com

SPAS

St Lucia is something of a spa destination, with some excellent establishments island-wide offering a wealth of rejuvenating treatments.
Kai Mer Spa ⓐ Coconut Bay Hotel, Vieux Fort ⓣ 459 6000 ⓦ www.cbay resort.com
Lapli Spa ⓐ Discovery Hotel, Marigot Bay ⓣ 458 5300 ⓦ www.discovery stlucia.com
Oasis ⓐ Le Sport Hotel, Cap Estate ⓣ 457 7856, ⓐ Cotton Bay Village, Cap Estate ⓣ 456 5700 and ⓐ Jalousie Plantation, Soufrière ⓣ 456 8048 ⓦ www.spasofstlucia.com
Red Lane Spa ⓐ Sandals Grande St Lucian, Rodney Bay ⓣ 726 3259 ⓦ www.sandals.com

WATERSPORTS

St Lucia's calm waters are ideal for watersports. Beachside operators at Rodney Bay and many of the larger hotels offer waterskiing, banana-boat rides or sailing on sunfish boats or hobie cats. Windsurfing and kite-surfing are best at breezy Anse des Sables (see page 65), where you can rent gear or take lessons.

Festivals & events

JANUARY
Nobel Laureate Week
Held in honour of St Lucia's two Nobel Laureates, Derek Walcott and Sir Arthur Lewis, who were both born on 23 January (though in different years), with everything from lectures and poetry readings to concerts and theatre performances staged over a week around their joint birthday. Sir Arthur Lewis died in 1991, but fellow Laureate Derek Walcott is usually on the island to participate in the celebration.

FEBRUARY
Independence Day (public holiday)
St Lucia was granted its independence from Britain on 22 February 1979, and the event is celebrated island-wide. Castries is the centre of the action, with street parades and concerts to mark this important date in the island's history.

APRIL
St Lucia Golf Open
Held at the St Lucia Country Club Golf Course on the first weekend after Easter (so precise dates vary), this two-day open tournament attracts players from most of the neighbouring islands, as well as the local hotshots, all keen to be picked for the OECS (Organisation of Eastern Caribbean States) team, which then plays in a regional championship.

MAY
St Lucia Jazz
Easily the biggest event in the island's events calendar, St Lucia holds one of the best and most popular of the region's many jazz festivals, attracting big international names such as Rihanna, Dionne Warwick, Anita Baker and John Legend alongside the cream of Caribbean talent. Spread over ten days, concerts are staged all over the island, culminating in the headline acts taking to the stage in the open-air setting of Pigeon

◔ *Colourful costumes at Carnival*

Island National Landmark. As the festival is so popular, hotels and flights can be in short supply – book well ahead, and expect to pay a premium. Visit Ⓦ www.stluciajazz.org for more information.

Desmond Skeete Memorial

This open golf tournament, held in honour of a former minister of tourism, runs alongside the Jazz festival, and features the Jazz on the Green reception as well as the sporting action.

JUNE
Fishermen's Feast (Fete Pêche)

Dennery is one of St Lucia's main fishing ports, and this big event, staged on the last weekend of June, is dedicated to St Peter, patron saint of fishermen. Church services are followed by the blessing of decorated fishing boats and a beach party.

JULY
Carnival

Held between May and the end of July, Carnival kicks off with competitions to crown the year's best soca and calypso singers, and the Carnival Queen beauty pageant. The festival's climax is the all-day Parade of the Bands, when thousands of skimpily costumed revellers dance through the streets of Castries on the Monday and Tuesday, with music supplied by steel bands and banks of speakers aboard flatbed trucks. For night owls, there's also Jouvert, held Sunday night and into the early hours of the Monday morning, in which revellers smear themselves in mud and body paint and take to the streets. Throughout the carnival period, fêtes – or outdoor parties – take place at the weekends. Visit Ⓦ www.stlucia.org for more information.

AUGUST
Emancipation Day & National Heroes Day (public holiday)

This holiday falls on 1 August, marking the day the British abolished slavery in 1834, with parades island-wide in remembrance of the freeing of the slaves and of the island's national heroes.

OCTOBER
Jounen Kwéyòl
A month of events to celebrate Creole (*Kwéyòl*) culture (see page 121), with the main celebration on the Sunday closest to International Creole Day (28 October), when four communities around the island host activities such as demonstrations of traditional craft-making and dance, while coal-pots on open fires bubble with delicious Creole specialities such as bouillon, a one-pot meat stew. For more information, contact the Folk Research Centre on ☎ 453 1477.

NOVEMBER
Atlantic Rally for Cruisers
The finish of this transatlantic rally at Rodney Bay Marina is marked with concerts and parties to congratulate the crews that complete the crossing.

DECEMBER
National Day – Festival of Lights and Renewal
Christmas lights in all the island's villages are turned on.

CALENDAR OF PUBLIC HOLIDAYS
New Year's Day 1 & 2 January
Independence Day 22 February
Good Friday & Easter Monday March/April
Labour Day 1 May
Whit Monday 7th Monday after Easter
Corpus Christi June
Emancipation Day & National Heroes Day 1 August
Thanksgiving Day 1st Monday in October
National Day 13 December
Christmas Day & Boxing Day 25 & 26 December

❍ *Pointing you in the right direction along the west-coast highway*

PRACTICAL INFORMATION
Tips & advice

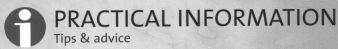

Accommodation

Most St Lucian hotels quote rates in US dollars. The symbol after the name of each hotel indicates the cost per night of a double room for two people including breakfast.

£ under US$160 **££** US$160–250 **£££** over US$250

Note that most hotels add an 8 per cent government tax and 10 per cent service charge to their rates.

CASTRIES

Auberge Seraphine £ Just outside Castries and backing on to the waters of the Vigie Marina, this intimate little place has appealing rooms with outdoor patio, as well as a pool and a good restaurant and bar. ⓐ Vielle Bay, Pointe Seraphine ① 453 2073 Ⓦ www.aubergeseraphine.com

🔺 *Some hotels have fantastic views over the Pitons*

Windjammer Landing £££ Fabulous location on white-sand Labrelotte Bay, plus sweeping sea views, with suites and apartments, pool, watersports, several restaurants and bars, and nightly entertainment. ⓐ Labrelotte Bay ☎ 546 9000 Ⓦ www.windjammer-landing.com

EAST COAST

Fox Grove Inn £ A lovely retreat on the quiet east coast, surrounded by banana plantations and with great sea views. Rooms are comfortable and appealing, and there's a pool, renowned restaurant and gardens. ⓐ Mon Repos ☎ 455 3271 Ⓦ www.foxgroveinn.com

MARIGOT BAY & THE WEST COAST

Marigot Beach Resort ££ Right on the bay's best beach, this classic hotel has pleasant rooms overlooking the sea (some with kitchenette) as well as villas. Big pool, restaurant and bar, and great watersports facilities. ⓐ Marigot Bay ☎ 451 4974 Ⓦ www.marigotbeachclub.com

Discovery £££ Ranged down a lush hillside, this resort blends Caribbean architecture with modern style. The rooms and suites have bay views, and facilities – from dining to the pool and spa – are exemplary. ⓐ Marigot Bay ☎ 458 5300 Ⓦ www.discoverystlucia.com

Ti Kaye Village £££ A lovely remote location overlooking a fabulous beach with excellent snorkelling just offshore, this is a wonderful retreat. Scattered down a hillside, rooms and cottages have hammocks on the veranda and pleasant décor; some have plunge pools and outdoor shower. ⓐ Anse Cochon ☎ 456 8101 Ⓦ www.tikaye.com

THE NORTHERN TIP

Cap Maison £££ Upmarket hotel above Smugglers' Cove beach, with a range of luxurious rooms and suites with balconies overlooking the sea; some have their own pool or whirlpool. Facilities include several restaurants, a spa and a watersports centre. ⓐ Smugglers' Cove Drive, Cap Estate ☎ 457 8670 Ⓦ www.capmaison.com

Cotton Bay £££ St Lucia's newest place to stay, and one of its most exclusive, this upmarket villa resort has three restaurants, a beautiful pool, plenty of land and water activities and a spa. ⓐ Cas en Bas, Cap Estate ⓣ 456 5700 ⓦ www.cottonbayvillage.com

Le Sport £££ This is an upmarket all-inclusive resort with an emphasis on healthy living. The spa is one of the island's best, and activities include yoga, t'ai chi, fencing and hiking. The pool, beach and restaurant are top-notch. ⓐ Cap Estate ⓣ 457 7800 ⓦ www.thebodyholiday.com

RODNEY BAY

Coco Palm £ Handsome resort with spacious rooms, all mod cons and lovely antique-style furnishings. Huge pool, spa and a good restaurant. ⓐ Rodney Bay Boulevard ⓣ 456 2800 ⓦ www.coco-resorts.com

Rex Royal £ Somewhat dated but charming nonetheless, right on the best part of Reduit Beach and with a large pool, two restaurants, spa and gym. Rooms have balconies with sea views. ⓐ Reduit Beach Avenue, Rodney Bay ⓣ 452 9999 ⓦ www.rexresorts.com

Bay Gardens Beach Resort £££ On Reduit Beach, and a great bet for families, with self-catering suites as well as ordinary rooms. There's a pool and restaurant, plus a spa, fitness centre and dive shop. ⓐ Reduit Beach Avenue, Rodney Bay ⓣ 457 8500 ⓦ www.baygardensresorts.com

SOUFRIÈRE

La Haut Plantation ££ Overlooking Soufrière and Petit Piton, set in lovely gardens and with a spectacular infinity pool. With a restaurant and bar, rooms are smart, with all mod cons, and some have kitchenettes. ⓐ Soufrière ⓣ 459 7008 ⓦ www.lahaut.com

Anse Chastanet £££ With amazing views of the Pitons, this is a gorgeous property with a range of stylish and luxurious rooms. Spa, dive shop (great snorkelling off the brown-sand beach), pool and excellent restaurant on-site make this an excellent place to stay. ⓐ Anse Chastanet, Soufrière ☎ 459 7000 ⓦ www.ansechastanet.com

Jade Mountain £££ Perhaps the most architecturally unusual hotel in St Lucia, with a stunning design of greenery-swathed columns and bridges leading to the semi-open-air suites, all of which have private infinity pools and afford fabulous views over the sea to the Pitons. Hugely romantic and super-luxurious, with a top-of-the-range spa to boot. Guests also have access to the beach at Anse Chastanet, just below. ⓐ Anse Chastanet ☎ 459 4000 ⓦ www.jademountainstlucia.com

Jalousie Plantation £££ A unique location between the two Pitons, this all-inclusive resort spreads up the hillside from a white-sand beach. Facilities range from a spa to a pool, tennis courts and watersports, including scuba and snorkelling in the marine park. ⓐ Val des Pitons, Soufrière ☎ 456 8000 ⓦ www.jalousieplantation.com

Ladera £££ Perhaps the most romantic hotel on the island, this unforgettable place offers rooms with no walls that afford fabulous Pitons views, as well as private plunge pools and artistic décor. Wonderful on-site restaurant (see page 63), spa and excellent service. ⓐ Soufrière ☎ 459 7323 ⓦ www.ladera.com

VIEUX FORT
Juliette's Lodge £ Close to the airport and Anse des Sables, this is a well-run place and perfect if you want to kite-surf. Rooms are comfortable and modern, with lovely views to the Maria Islands. There's a pool, bar and restaurant. ⓐ Beanfield, Vieux Fort ☎ 454 5300 ⓦ www.julietteslodge.com

Coconut Bay £££ The largest hotel in the south, this sprawling all-inclusive is the island's best bet for families, with excellent facilities including a water park with lazy river and slides, kids' club for ages 3–12, paintball zone and three pools. There are also three restaurants and a nightclub. ⓐ Vieux Fort ☎ 459 6000 ⓦ www.cbayresort.com

Preparing to go

GETTING THERE

Many people travelling to St Lucia visit on a package holiday that includes flight and accommodation, and as operators usually have deals with hotels on the island, this can work out a lot less expensive than booking both your travel and your hotel yourself. Even if you want to explore the island independently, you might still want to consider booking a package, as it's still possible to make savings by staying in the pre-booked accommodation for part of the trip and then branching out on your own. In terms of scheduled flights, British Airways (☎ 0844 493 0787 🅦 www.ba.com) flies from Gatwick on Tuesday, Wednesday, Thursday, Saturday and Sunday, while Virgin Atlantic (☎ 0870 380 2007 🅦 www.virgin-atlantic.com) has a service from Gatwick on Sunday, Tuesday and Friday; both also offer packages as well as flights. Most travel agents can arrange a flight or package for you, and

TRAVEL INSURANCE

Taking out travel insurance is strongly recommended. There are excellent deals to be had if you shop around, ranging from short breaks to annual cover. However, many of the basic options exclude certain activities, and if you are planning to go scuba diving or snorkelling, ride a motorbike or engage in other pastimes deemed higher risk, then you will almost certainly need to pay a little extra. Medical facilities in St Lucia are relatively limited, and while local practitioners can deal with minor complaints or injuries, it's important to ensure your policy covers air evacuation in the event of a serious illness or accident. You should also get one that has adequate coverage for loss or theft of your belongings, and if you're taking expensive items such as camcorders or a laptop, make sure that their value doesn't exceed the per-item limit.

you can also book by calling or visiting the websites of the airlines above. Flying time from Gatwick to St Lucia is around eight hours. You can also fly to St Lucia from other Caribbean islands; LIAT (📞 1 268 480 5601 🌐 www.liat.com) is the main regional operator.

Many people are aware that air travel emits CO_2, which contributes to climate change. You may be interested in the possibility of lessening the environmental impact of your flight through the charity **Climate Care**, which offsets your CO_2 by funding environmental projects around the world. Visit 🌐 www.jpmorganclimatecare.com

TOURISM AUTHORITY

The **St Lucia Tourist Board** has its main office in the Sureline Building, inconveniently located north of Castries on the road to Gros Islet (📞 452 4094 or 452 5698); there's another office in Soufrière on the waterfront (📞 459 7419 🕐 08.00–16.00 Mon–Fri, 08.00–12.00 Sat, closed Sun). There are also information booths at both airports, and at the Pointe Seraphine and La Place Carenage malls in Castries. There are also offices within embassies and consulates overseas, including the UK and US; for details, visit the website, which has lots of information on the island and its attractions. 🌐 www.stlucia.org

BEFORE YOU LEAVE

St Lucia's tropical climate means it's best to pack light clothing in natural fabrics. Include some long-sleeved tops and trousers to protect against mosquitoes and cool evening breezes; insect repellent is also a must. Though most people dress casually, it's worth bringing something smart if you plan on eating out a lot. In terms of sunblock, those with fair skins should start with at least a factor 30; and it's always sensible to stay out of the sun between 12.00 and mid-afternoon, when the rays are at their hottest. You can buy sunblock in St Lucia, though you may not get all the brands you would at home. You should also make sure that you bring adequate supplies of any prescription medicines that you take regularly. Other packing essentials include a converter plug for any appliances that you bring with you, and a hat to protect against the often-fierce sun –

though you can pick up the latter from one of innumerable trinket shops island-wide.

ENTRY FORMALITIES

All visitors to St Lucia must present a valid passport on arrival, and fill in an immigration form detailing where they'll be staying. You must also have an onward ticket and proof of sufficient funds to cover your trip. Citizens of the US, UK, Germany, France, Italy and Spain can enter the country for up to 42 days without a visa. No vaccination certificates are required for entry to St Lucia unless you're travelling from a country where yellow fever is endemic. Visitors over the age of 18 are allowed to import 200 cigarettes, 50 cigars or 250 g of loose tobacco and one litre of wine or spirits.

MONEY

St Lucia's currency is the Eastern Caribbean dollar (abbreviated as EC$). You'll often see goods and services priced in US dollars, too, and you can use US dollars to make payments. Cash and traveller's cheques can be exchanged at most banks, and ATMs that accept foreign cards are commonplace; note that they dispense EC dollars only. Most hotels and tourist-oriented restaurants and bars accept credit cards, and you can also get cash advances on debit or credit cards at most ATMs.

CLIMATE

St Lucia's climate is tropical, with temperatures ranging from 21–32°C (70–90°F). The weather is at its most pleasant during the high season (December to April), with plenty of sunshine, cool breezes in the evenings and only the occasional rain shower. This is also the best time to visit, as all the hotels, restaurants and attractions are open for business; the downside, though, is that things can get busy and accommodation rates are at their highest. The period around the St Lucia Jazz Festival in May is also busy, and some hotels jack up their rates at this time. During the summer months, the days can get oppressively hot and humid, while the rainy season lasts from June to

November, which also roughly coincides with the annual hurricane season. You may get long showers and cloud cover during the day at this time, but it's rare for the skies to open for days on end, and there's usually some sun each day.

BAGGAGE ALLOWANCES

Most airlines will allow you to travel with one checked bag of 23 kg (50 lb) for free, and a single piece of hand luggage; some allow a laptop bag or handbag as well. It's usually possible to pay for an additional 23-kg (50-lb) bag as well. You have to pay an excess charge for checked bags over 23 kg (50 lb), but few airlines will accept pieces that weigh over 32 kg (70 lb) for health and safety reasons. Continuing restrictions on liquids in hand luggage mean that you can only carry liquids or gels in containers of under 100 ml (3½ fl oz), and all liquids must be separated from the rest of your things in a clear, ziplock bag. As baggage allowances change frequently, however, it's best to treat the above information as a guide only, and check with your airline before you travel.

During your stay

AIRPORTS

Hewanorra International Airport is just outside Vieux Fort, in the south of the island and on the opposite side of St Lucia to Rodney Bay (meaning you need to set aside at least an hour to make the journey if you're staying in the north of the island). Buses (see page 120) run up the relatively fast east-coast highway (rather than the winding west-coast route) to Castries, Rodney Bay and all points north, and there are also services up the west coast to Soufrière, Anse La Raye and Marigot Bay, but it's far easier to take a taxi. Taxis are readily available, and there are car-rental outlets at the airport, too. If you are visiting on a package deal, transfers to and from your hotel are usually included. Flights from other Caribbean islands arrive and depart from George F L Charles Airport, just north of Castries on Vigie Peninsula. Buses run from here into the capital, and there is a taxi rank and car-rental booths.

> ### DEPARTURE TAX
> All passengers over 12 years old must pay a departure tax of EC\$68 on leaving the island. However, it's usually included in ticket prices; check with your airline.

COMMUNICATIONS

There are telephone booths all over the island, which accept either coins or cards, available from pharmacies and supermarkets. Given the prevalence of mobile phones, however, they're not always well maintained these days. In terms of mobiles, you can roam with your home tri-band phone on one of several local networks; if you plan on making a lot of calls, it's cheaper to buy a local SIM card and add credit as you go. The main providers are Lime and Digicel.

There are post offices (or sub-offices) in all of St Lucia's towns and larger villages. They open Monday to Friday 08.15 to 16.30, though the Rodney Bay one also opens on Saturday from 09.00 to 12.00. Postcards

TELEPHONING ST LUCIA
From Europe 00 + 1 + 758 + number
From the US & Canada 011 + 1 + 758 + number
From Australia 0011 + 1 + 758 + number
From New Zealand 00 + 1 + 758 + number
From South Africa 00 + 1 + 758 + number

TELEPHONING ABROAD
(Omit the first zero from the area code)
UK 011 + 44 + area code and number
US & Canada 1 + area code and number
Australia 011 + 61 + area code and number
New Zealand 011 + 64 + area code and number
South Africa 011 + 27 + area code and number

cost EC$0.65 to the UK and US, and EC$0.70 to the rest of Europe; stamps are available from post offices and pharmacies; some hotel gift shops also sell them.

Most hotels now offer Internet access, with either Wi-Fi or terminals for guests' use or both; many bars and restaurants in tourist areas also have wireless access. You'll also find Internet cafés in Castries, Marigot Bay, Rodney Bay, Soufrière and Vieux Fort, offering inexpensive and fast access.

CUSTOMS

Despite the raunchy dancing you see at Carnival and the generally relaxed atmosphere, St Lucia is a fairly conservative country, with the majority of the population practising Christians. While the locals certainly know how to have a good time, public drunkenness and lewd behaviour are frowned upon.

DRESS CODES

Topless sunbathing is illegal in St Lucia, and though some visitors do try and get an all-over tan on secluded beaches, it may well cause offence to locals. It's also best to keep swimwear for the beach; parading around the supermarket in your bikini will be considered impolite and will certainly earn you some withering stares.

With regard to dress codes, the smartest restaurants require men to wear a jacket, long trousers and covered shoes; evening dress isn't required for women, but you may want to bring a smart sundress.

ELECTRICITY

Electric current is 220 volts/50 Hz. Most hotels have UK-style three-pin sockets, but some have two-pin round or flat sockets that are 110 volts/60 Hz. Most hotels have adaptors which they can lend out to guests, but as supplies are limited, it makes sense to bring adaptors with you if you'll need to use them regularly, such as for charging a mobile phone.

EMERGENCIES

In a medical emergency, call ☎ 911. The main hospital is the Victoria in Castries (☎ 452 2421) but there's also St Jude's in Vieux Fort (☎ 454 6041). All hotels will be able to recommend a doctor or a dentist. There are pharmacies island-wide, with the best ones in JQ Mall, Rodney Bay, and Gablewoods Mall, Castries.

The police HQ is on Bridge Street in Castries (☎ 452 2854).

In the event of any problems, UK residents can contact:
British High Commission ⓐ 2nd Floor, Francis Compton Building, Castries Waterfront ☎ 452 2484 ⓔ britishhc@candw.lc

There are no Irish, American, Australian, New Zealand or South African consulates on St Lucia.

EMERGENCY NUMBERS
Ambulance ☎ 911
Fire ☎ 911
Police ☎ 999

GETTING AROUND

By car

Driving in St Lucia is relatively straightforward. St Lucians drive on the left. Roads are adequate, though there is the odd phenomenal pothole away from main routes, and the west-coast highway is characterised by its switchback turns and up-and-down hills – take medication if you tend to get car sick. Signage is fairly good, but if you do get lost, the best plan is to stop and ask someone local. However, most places you'll want to go are on – or signposted off – the coastal highways that run down the west and east coasts.

Castries can seem a little hairy at first, but if you're driving through town from the north to reach the west or east coasts, or vice versa, you'll find the route via the Millennium Highway (rather then Morne Fortune) well signposted. The turn-off from the highway to the inland road that cuts through to the east coast is also well marked. On-street parking is inadvisable in Castries, as ticketing and even towing are likely; instead, use the inexpensive multi-storey car park on your left as you enter town from the north. In terms of safety, it's important to drive defensively and wear seat belts in both the back and front at all times. As well as keeping an eye out for potholes or animals on the roads, bear in mind that local drivers can often seem a bit reckless, speeding wherever possible and attempting manoeuvres such as overtaking on corners. Don't be tempted to keep up; pull over and let such drivers pass as soon as possible.

Car hire

There are car-rental outlets throughout the island, with the main concentration in Castries and Rodney Bay, and booths at both airports. To drive on the island you need a valid licence from your home country, and most agencies will also require you to be over 25. If you don't have an international driving licence, you'll also need to purchase a local drivers' permit, which costs EC$54 and can be arranged by the rental company. It's a good idea to pay a little extra for the Collision Damage Waiver, which means you're not liable for all of the damage should you be involved in an accident (usually the first US$750 rather than US$1,500).

Reliable companies include:

Car Total (car and jeep rental) ⓐ Balata, Castries ☏ 450 2414
ⓦ www.cartotalslu.com

H&B Car Rental ⓐ Rodney Bay Village, Rodney Bay ☏ 452 0872
ⓦ www.handbcarrental.com

Public transport

St Lucia's buses are actually privately owned and operated minibuses,
running from the main bus park in Castries (just behind the market) to
all points in the island. The main routes travel along the west-coast
highway down to Soufrière, and along the east coast highway to Vieux
Fort. You can stop a bus (and alight) anywhere along the route – just
stick out your hand to hail one – and fares are ridiculously cheap. Though
they tend to be packed with passengers and speed along at what might
feel like an alarming rate, they're an excellent way to meet locals and
get from A to B without breaking the bank.

⬤ *Water-taxi: a perfect way to explore the coast*

Taxis & water-taxis

Taxis are easy to come by on St Lucia, with legions of drivers working the resort areas. Stick to official taxis with the red 'TH' plate. All taxis are unmetered, so you should always agree on the fare before you start a journey.

Water-taxis are a fun alternative for exploring the beaches around Soufrière (boats leave from the main dock) or travelling between Castries harbour and Rodney Bay; again, negotiate the fare before you set out.

HEALTH, SAFETY & CRIME

St Lucia poses few health risks to travellers. No vaccinations are needed, and the water is chlorinated, but though it's theoretically safe to drink, it's probably best to stick to bottled water. In terms of food safety, standards are pretty high, and there's no reason to avoid things like salads, ice cream, or ice in drinks.

CREOLE CULTURE

St Lucia's official language is English, but locals also speak Creole patois (*Kwéyòl*), which uses some French pronunciation but which is pretty much incomprehensible to outsiders. A proper language in its own right rather than a broken form of French or English, with rules of grammar and syntax, *Kwéyòl* is very much alive and kicking in St Lucia – you'll hear it in radio broadcasts as well as on the streets, and local scholars have published a *Kwéyòl* Bible and dictionary.

Some key phrases include:

Bon jou – hello

Orevwa – goodbye

Souplé – Please

Mèsi – Thank you

Sa ka fét? – How are you?

Minor ailments are best treated at private clinics, or by the doctor on call that your hotel will be able to recommend. Public hospitals are poorly equipped in comparison to those in the UK or US, but standards of care are good. However, it's important to take out a travel insurance policy that covers you for evacuation in the unlikely event of you becoming seriously ill (see page 112).

Crime levels are low in St Lucia, but the occasional robbery does of course occur, and you should take the usual common-sense precautions. Don't carry large amounts of cash or wear expensive jewellery or watches, and always store valuables in hotel safety-deposit boxes. Avoid walking alone on unlit beaches at night, and keep your wits about you when exploring Castries, where pickpocketing is not unknown.

Should you be unlucky enough to be the victim of a robbery, you must make a police report in order to make an insurance claim. St Lucian police are not the most efficient in the world, though they are generally helpful and courteous. Policemen and -women are easily recognisable by their blue shirts; senior officers wear a khaki uniform.

Bear in mind that, though you may be offered it on the beaches or in bars, marijuana (ganja in St Lucia) is illegal here, and penalties for possession are severe.

MEDIA

St Lucia has several newspapers: the *Star* (Ⓦ www.stluciastar.com), which comes out on a Monday, Wednesday and Saturday; *The Voice* (Ⓦ www.thevoiceslu.com), which comes out on a Tuesday, Thursday and Saturday; and the weekly *Mirror. Tropical Traveller* (Ⓦ www.tropical traveller.com) is published monthly and available for free in hotels and restaurants; it has articles on hotels, restaurants and island attractions, as does the annual *Paradise St Lucia* (Ⓦ www.paradisestlucia.com).

Radio stations include Radio St Lucia (97.3 and 97.7 FM), Helen FM (100.1, 100.3 and 103.5 FM) and RCI (101.1 FM), all with a mix of news and Caribbean music.

Most hotels have cable or satellite TV that receive innumerable American channels and BBC World News. There are also local information channels with programmes on St Lucian restaurants and attractions which are worth watching.

OPENING HOURS

Shops and offices tend to open Monday to Friday from 10.00 to 16.00, and shops also open on Saturday from 10.00 until 13.00; some close for an hour for lunch. Banks open Monday to Thursday from 08.00 to 14.00 and Friday from 08.00 to 17.00. Banks at the Rodney Bay Marina complex also open on Saturday from 08.00 until 12.00.

RELIGION

Some 80 per cent of St Lucians are Roman Catholic, and there are churches in almost every village of any size across the island. Your hotel can advise about service times should you wish to attend church.

SMOKING LAWS

There are no laws pertaining to smoking in St Lucia, and it's fine to light up in most restaurants, bars and clubs. Some indoor, air-conditioned places have an outdoor smoking area, however.

TIME DIFFERENCES

St Lucia is four hours behind the UK's Greenwich Mean Time, and one hour ahead of Eastern Standard Time in the US.

TIPPING

It's customary to tip waiters between 10 per cent and 15 per cent, though a service charge is added to most bills. It's also usual to tip taxi drivers, and bellhops who help with luggage in hotels. You might also want to leave something for your chambermaid at the end of your stay.

TOILETS

Public toilets are pretty much non-existent in St Lucia. Your best option is to head for a tourist-oriented restaurant or bar, or a fast-food chain, where facilities are likely to be clean and serviceable.

TRAVELLERS WITH DISABILITIES

There's not much provision for travellers with disabilities in St Lucia. Though the newer hotels have made themselves accessible for wheelchairs with ramps and the like, the island can be a challenge in terms of getting around. Pavements – where they exist – often have high kerbs, and the surface tends to be very uneven. Access to buses can also be near impossible for wheelchair users. Though awareness of disability issues is not that high in St Lucia, you will nevertheless find that people are more than willing to help with mobility. For local support and information, contact the **St Lucia National Council of and for Persons with Disabilities** (ⓐ La Toc Road, Castries ⓣ 453 1539). International organisations and companies offering travel advice and tips for people with disabilities include **Disability Travel** (UK) (ⓣ 020 8731 2111 ⓦ www.disabilitytravel.co.uk) and **Accessible Journeys** (USA) (ⓣ 610 521 0339 ⓦ www.disabilitytravel.com).

ACKNOWLEDGEMENTS

Thomas Cook Publishing wishes to thank the photographers, picture libraries and other organisations, to whom the copyright belongs, for the photographs in this book.

Alamy page 61 (Susan E Degginger)
Dexter Lewis pages 12–13, 30, 34, 43, 50, 57, 58, 62, 66, 73, 74, 79, 84, 95, 99, 100, 108, 120
Dreamstime.com page 8 (Michael Mattner)
iStockphoto page 41 (Sarah8000)
Photoshot page 32 (Cuboimages)
Polly Thomas pages 5, 15, 18, 21, 24, 37, 45, 68, 70, 77, 81, 86, 89, 91, 104, 107
Wikimedia Commons pages 11 (Jayen 466), 48 (Mjr74)

For CAMBRIDGE PUBLISHING MANAGEMENT LIMITED:
Project editors: Jennifer Jahn & Rosalind Munro
Layout: Donna Pedley
Proofreaders: Rosalind Munro & Cath Senker

Send your thoughts to
books@thomascook.com

- **Found a beach bar, peaceful stretch of sand or must-see sight that we don't feature?**

- **Like to tip us off about any information that needs a little updating?**

- **Want to tell us what you love about this handy, little guidebook and, more importantly, how we can make it even handier?**

Then here's your chance to tell all! Send us ideas, discoveries and recommendations today and then look out for your valuable input in the next edition of this title.

Email to the above address or write to:
pocket guides Series Editor, Thomas Cook Publishing, PO Box 227, Unit 9, Coningsby Road, Peterborough PE3 8SB, UK.

Thomas Cook **pocket guides**

PARIS

Your travelling companion since 1873

Thomas
Cook